Miracles — Eyewitness to the Miraculous

by
R.W. Schambach

All Scripture quotations are from the *King James Version* of the Bible.

Miracles — Eyewitness to the Miraculous
ISBN 0-89274-811-7
Copyright © 1993 by R. W. Schambach
P. O. Box 9009
Tyler, Texas 75711

Contents

Introduction
by "Winn" Schambach

Most of my life I have heard the stories that Brother Schambach tells. Some of the miracles that you are about to read, I have heard a hundred times!

I will read this book right along with you. No matter how often I hear my husband tell them, they are always fresh. They demonstrate the miracle-working power of God.

Brother Schambach began his evangelistic ministry in 1955 while working with renowned evangelist Brother A.A. Allen, from whom he received valuable training. This prepared him for the work God had called him to.

In 1959 Brother Schambach began his ministry with a crusade in Newark, New Jersey, where signs and wonders followed. The revival lasted for six months! Reluctant to leave the new converts and friends, he founded a church, Newark Miracle Temple.

This pattern was repeated as Brother Schambach traveled across the East. Later on, other Miracle Temple churches were established in Philadelphia, Chicago and Brooklyn. His reputation became that of one of the great "tent evangelists."

Across the country, Brother Schambach held great revivals under his ministry's tent, where virtually thousands of lost souls came to Christ. Thousands more received physical, financial and emotional miracles. Brother Schambach's radio broadcasts and television program soon became powerful extensions of the ministry with which God had blessed him.

Today the same signs and wonders still follow Brother Schambach's work. The pages of this book relate some of those miracles.

Many of the miracles you are going to read in this book took place while I was standing right beside Brother Schambach — I am an eyewitness to them. For instance, you will read about the seventeen deaf and dumb brothers and sisters in Africa. All of them were healed and began to hear and speak in one miracle service!

It is exciting to be there when God's power is at work. Because Brother Schambach is a powerful story teller, you will feel as if you were really there with him. He brings the stories to life, making them vivid and alive.

I have watched little children sit spell-bound with their eyes wide and their mouths open, as Brother Schambach tells a story. He has a unique and fascinating way of expressing himself.

I hope that the miracle stories included in this book will build your faith and inspire you as you continue to walk with the Lord.

1

What Mohammed Couldn't Do

When I pastored a church in the early 1950s, we sponsored a missionary in India by paying his salary. He spent thirty years there — thirty long years.

On one occasion, he told me something that discouraged me from even supporting him. He said he had spent thirty years in India and had never seen one Mohammedan born again. I said, "What kind of investment am I making? We are investing money and keeping that man in India to preach the Gospel and not one soul has been saved. It is time to rearrange our priorities." So I went to India to find out what was going on.

The first time I visited India in 1956, I preached to 50,000 people. I visited all the market places. I saw beggars, blind folks and people who couldn't walk. I have never seen so many sick people. India is one of the poorest nations in the world with so many homeless, penniless people.

We invested thousands of dollars to build a structure that protected the people from the hot sun so that they could hear the Gospel. On that opening day, I was so thrilled. I preached for two hours and my interpreter translated for two hours — for a total of four hours. They wanted me to go on. When I gave the altar call, I was so disappointed. I had preached to 50,000 people, and not one soul had come to accept Jesus.

My mind went back to the missionary and I said, "Oh, Lord." But I knew God called us to do more than just preach the Word. He called us to demonstrate the Gospel.

Although no one came forward to accept Christ, and the crowd was obviously ready for the benediction, I said, "I am not done now. God says that signs follow His Word. I did what God called me to do, now I am going to let God do what He said He was going to do."

I invited three people from the audience to come forward — they were beggars. I knew who they were. One was blind, one was deaf and dumb and the other was a crippled woman who had never walked upright. She walked in a horizontal position on the heels of her feet and the heels of her hands. She had a disease that hindered her from standing upright.

Fifty thousand people were watching.

I laid hands on the blind woman first. I said, "In the name of Jesus, I command these blind eyes to see." Instantly, God opened her eyes and she ran through the audience, shouting in her own tongue, "I can see! I can see!"

I went to the deaf mute and put my fingers in his ears and my thumb on his tongue. I said, "In the name of Jesus, I command this deaf and dumb spirit to come out!" Instantly, the spirit responded and the man started speaking English within a few minutes. He didn't know his own language. He had been a deaf mute but God had opened his ears and loosened his tongue.

It came time to pray for the crippled woman. I said, "Now I am going to lay hands on this woman in the name of Mohammed. I am going to give him equal time." My interpreter did not want to translate this statement. I said, "You do what I tell you to do, Mister. You are my interpreter. I am the man of God."

Not one person in the audience expected her to get up, because they knew Mohammed was dead. I said, "Now, that is the difference between the god you serve and the God I serve. I didn't come here to put your god down; I came to lift mine up. You visit your shrine. I visit mine, but mine is empty because He is no longer there. That is the difference between the tombs. I came to let you know my Jesus is not dead — He is alive, and He is the same today as He was yesterday."

I laid hands on the woman in the name of Mohammed and said, "Rise and walk, in the name of Mohammed." Someone asked me what I would have done if she had gotten up. I guess I would have converted.

But she didn't get up. So I said, "I am going to use the name that is above every name, the name of Jesus — the Lamb that was slain for the world. Jesus died for the people of India and for the whole world." The woman had never taken an upright step in fifty-eight years. I laid hands on her in the name of Jesus of Nazareth and said, "In the name of Jesus, rise and walk." She stood upright and walked for the first time in her life, because Jesus Christ is God!

Do you know what happened? The people in that crowd started jumping out of trees, and a mob came running towards me. I jumped behind my interpreter. I thought they were going to tar and feather me and run me out of their country. I never saw such an onslaught of people. They were yelling something at the top of their voice. I asked my interpreter, "What are they saying?"

He said, "They are hollering, 'Jesus is alive. Jesus is the Christ. Jesus is God.' They are coming to get saved." What a thrill! Not one of them came when I preached, but when they saw the demonstration of the Gospel, they came.

God has called the Church to demonstrate His power.

Aren't you glad He is alive today?

Then Philip went down to the city of Samaria, and preached Christ unto them. And the people

with one accord gave heed unto those things which Philip spake, hearing and seeing the miracles which he did.

Acts 8:5,6

2

It's Never Too Late

Some time ago, when I was in Seattle, Washington, I preached a message about Lazarus. The Bible says that Lazarus had been in the grave four days when Jesus finally came. Although it seemed as if He had arrived too late, He was right on time. He is never too late. In other words, it's never too late for a miracle.

Sometimes we put time limits on God. Mary and Martha were limited in their faith. They said to Jesus, **Lord, if thou hadst been here, my brother had not died** (John 11:21,32). They had forgotten that Jesus was Christ, the Son of God — Emmanuel: God with us. They had forgotten that Jesus is the Resurrection and the Life.

They didn't know that Jesus had intentionally waited. He wanted His followers to witness His miraculous power.

We should never try to figure out God's timetables. He is always on time. It's never too late.

After the service, a woman came to me and shoved a piece of paper into my hand. She said, "Now, I dare you to say it's not too late." Do you know what the paper was? A divorce paper, a final decree. She had just received it from the judge. It was final. The husband was gone. She looked me right in the eye and said again, "Now, I dare you to say it's not too late."

So I smiled and took her dare and said, "It's not too late."

She said, "What about that paper?"

I said, "You are looking at the wrong paper. My paper says, **What therefore God hath joined together, let not man put asunder** (Matt. 19:6). That is what I believe. How long have you been married?" She told me they had been married for twenty-seven years and had five children. I said, "That man has no business leaving you." I laid hands on her and said, "Holy Ghost, bring that rascal to his senses and save him. Don't bring him back home the way he is. Lord, save him and fill him with the Holy Ghost." I looked at the woman and said, "Go home and get ready for your husband. He is coming."

Of course, that was easy for me to say. I was leaving town. I am an evangelist. I can hit them and run. But in all honesty, I believed what I had said. My wife and I drove from Seattle to Philadelphia. When we got to Philly, I had a letter, from that woman, waiting for me. I opened it and the first lines said, "Dear Brother Schambach, God is never too late! God got a hold of that rascal, saved him and filled him with the Holy Ghost. The Lord brought him back home and we got married all over again."

That is the powerful aspect of faith. Take a stand of faith and say, "Devil, you are a liar. I am going to believe God for a miracle because He is going to turn this situation around." Speak faith. Speak to that mountain and that mountain has to obey your words. That is how you will experience the power of faith.

3
I Died Last Night

Our tent was standing on Sunrise Boulevard. It was one of the greatest revivals I have ever had — and a man died in the fourth row.

Immediately I went to him with my Bible. I wasn't going to let the devil kill anybody in my meeting. I commanded the devil to turn him loose. I called his spirit back into his body. There were no signs of life. I told my tent crew, "Come and take him behind the platform. No one is going to disturb my preaching." They took him there. Somehow we actually forgot about him.

I went to my hotel. At three-thirty in the morning, I sat straight up in bed and said, "Oh my, the dead man!" It was the first time I had thought about the incident since it happened.

The next night I returned to the tent. During the meeting I asked, "I want five of the happiest people here tonight to come up and tell us what you are happy about."

The dead man was the first in line!

I didn't recognize him. He was dressed up. I handed him the microphone and asked, "What are you happy about, brother?"

"Praise God!" he replied. "I died last night."

I thought, "What kind of nut do I have here?"

But he looked at me in a strange way and said, "Don't you remember me?"

"No, sir," I replied, "I don't remember you."

"You walked through four rows of chairs to get to me," he answered. "Brother Schambach, I had my fifth heart attack in your tent last night. Doctors told me if I had one more heart attack, it would kill me. My body was there but my spirit was gone. I saw you running back through those people. You called my spirit back into my body." Tears started running down his face. "I am so thankful you did that," he said, "because last night I was a sinner and I would have gone to hell if you hadn't stopped my spirit. My spirit came back into my body. I woke up behind that platform with a brand-new heart. I got saved and filled with the Holy Ghost last night. I went to my doctor today and he couldn't believe it."

The man shouted, "Jesus came into my heart last night and gave me a brand new heart. Hallelujah!"

His doctor had said to him, "Where are the other four scars on your heart?" He couldn't find the scars from the previous heart attacks. "You have the heart of a twenty-five year-old man."

Since that night, when God directs me, I don't hesitate to lay hands on any dead folks because they may not be saved. I would like them to be saved — saved from the burning flames of hell! That man was on his way to hell, but thank God, I got a hold of that spirit before the devil could claim him. God saved him and filled him with the Holy Ghost and with fire.

4
Hospital Riot in Newark

In 1960 God led me to anoint people with oil during the crusade services. Sometimes I asked them to take their shoes off so I could anoint their feet. Then, I anointed their hands and their head. I would just pour oil on them.

In those days, I gave a bottle of oil to fired-up believers and sent them out with it. "Go out there and find somebody who is sick," I would tell them. "Anoint them with oil so that they may be healed." In reality, oil is a symbol of the Holy Ghost.

Years ago, during a crusade in Newark, I laid hands on a young man. On this particular night, I gave him a bottle of oil and spoke those same words to him. I didn't see him for a few nights. Then, his best buddy came and told me, "He is in jail."

"Why is he in jail?" I demanded.

He said, "For listening to you."

Now, if he was in jail because of what I had said, I wanted to go bail him out. But the Lord said, "Leave him alone." That is the trouble with us. We want to mess things up. Just let the Lord have His way.

On the fifth night, the missing man came bouncing into our meeting. I never saw a young man on fire like he was. I prayed, "Lord, if jail will do that for folks, put all these people in jail." He was on fire!

I called him to the front and gave him the microphone. I wanted to hear what he had to say. As it turned out, I didn't get to preach that night.

He told the audience that when I gave him the oil and told him to find someone who was sick, he didn't even go home. He went to the nearest hospital — where the sick were. He didn't have a minister's card. He wasn't ordained. All he had was a bottle of oil and an edict from the preacher saying, "Go find somebody who is sick."

He went to the hospital. It happened to be the largest hospital in the city. Without signing in with the nurse, he headed straight for the elevator. When he reached the fifteenth floor, he got the bottle of oil out and started laying hands on the sick. He told everybody he laid hands on, "Get up and go home. God has healed you." He cleaned out the whole floor. Isn't that wild?

Those hospital patients had better sense than many church folks. They were going to do what the man of God told them to do, "Rise and walk."

After he got rid of the patients on that floor, he went down to the fourteenth floor. He was planning to anoint every patient in that hospital. Can you imagine folks going out the front door in slippers, pajamas and overcoats and the nurses asking what they were doing? "The doctor said we were healed and told us to go home!"

The young man went to the next floor. He walked into a ward of about 180 people. There were five doctors working with a woman who had just passed away. The young man didn't run in. He waited until the doctors left. After the last doctor left, they pulled a sheet over the woman.

He went to her and pulled the sheet back. Everybody in the ward was looking in his direction. As they watched, the young man poured oil on the woman and rebuked death in the name of Jesus. He called her spirit back into her body. Suddenly, the woman sputtered about a half a dozen times, got up and out of the bed. She started shouting and running around the hospital room.

This, of course, isn't my story. I am just telling you what the young man told us. It blew us away. Can you imagine the chaos that broke loose in that ward? When you go in with a bottle of oil and something like this happens, they aren't going to ask you what church you represent or for your credentials. There is a dead woman jumping and screaming.

Every patient on that floor was saying, "Hey! Bring that oil over here. If it will raise that woman from the dead, it will heal me!"

This is the reason I anoint people with oil. I want to stir up that gift in them. When you do what God has called you to do, you will have people crying out for help. There is a world out there waiting for the Church to come alive. Today is the day we can say, "Look out, devil!"

But the young man's story isn't over yet.

The nurses called the police. They arrested the young man. He was charged with disturbing the peace. He was guilty — yes, he was. He was disturbing the devil's peace. Don't you think it is about time the Church disturbs the devil's peace? The devil has been disturbing our peace all along.

The authorities put him in jail and left him there for four days. The judge was aggravated when he saw the paperwork on the case. He said, "Why would this man be kept in so long?" He told them to go and get him out. When they brought him, the judge apologized to him. "Your Honor, don't apologize," the young man said. "Jesus put me there."

The judge was mystified. "I have heard everything blamed on Him, but never this," he replied.

The young man told the judge the story I just told you. He said, "Your Honor, when they arrested me I still had some oil left. I have gone to all the prisoners and anointed them — every one of them. Just five minutes ago the jailer got saved. You got me out just as I finished."

The judge looked over his bench.

"Case dismissed," he said. Then he added, "Son, go get some more oil. God knows the Church isn't doing what He called it to do. Thank God there are young men being raised up to obey God."

I will never forget this story as long as I live. I tell it everywhere. Some folks don't believe it. But I just figure, they don't believe the Bible, why would they believe this?

Now you know why I anoint with oil.

5

Fortuneteller's Nightmare

I spent five years ministering with Brother A.A. Allen. Most of what I know today, I learned by his side. I describe my experience as that of an apprenticeship.

A.A. Allen cast out more devils accidentally than most ministers do on purpose. During those years with Brother Allen, I learned a few things about devils. As a result, I have cast out some devils in my day, too.

I had an interesting encounter with a devil in Pennsylvania.

My wife's father had a hunting cabin in the mountains. One weekend he asked me to go there with him. I had the weekend off, so I said, "All right, Pop, I will go with you." After the second day, I could no longer take it. I was tired of preaching to squirrels. By Saturday night, I was looking for some excitement. I am used to a Holy Ghost night on Saturday! In the woods, in a log cabin, killing flies was the only excitement there was. So I said, "Pop, I am getting out of here."

There was a small town of about 375 nearby where a street fair was underway. I saw a number of little tents and something about a tent attracts me. One of the tents had a crystal ball in it. In the front there was a sign that said, "Fortunes Told."

I headed for the fortuneteller. I wanted some excitement, and I was going to get it. I had found a devil.

I saw the fortuneteller come out of her tent. Dressed in her attire she played the part perfectly. She wore a gypsy scarf and long earrings that hung down to her shoulders.

Her eyes caught mine and she froze. My eyes were glued to hers. I headed right to her. When I got close enough, she spoke — or rather, the demon inside her spoke. She took the tent curtain, draped it around her and said, "I know you, you man of God."

I said, "I know you, too, you devil." I was telling the truth. I do know him!

She quickly drew the curtain closer to her and stayed inside the tent. I leaned in and said, "You aren't telling any fortunes tonight, you devil. You have been tormenting God's people, but *now I am going to torment you!*"

And I did.

Acts 19:15 says, **And the evil spirit answered and said, Jesus I know, and Paul I know; but who are ye?** You need to be so full of the Holy Ghost that the devil knows who you are. God never intended for us to run away from the devil. God intended for us to run after him!

6
Neff Baby Miracle

There was a coal miner who had a precious little baby boy. He and his wife had agreed that he was going to be in the delivery room when this child was born. They had two other children, but he wanted to witness the birth of this one.

It is a good thing he was in the delivery room because there were complications. The doctor panicked and told the husband, "Press down on your wife's stomach and force that baby out."

Of course, the husband didn't know about delivering babies, and he was also panicking. But he did what the doctor said. He pushed down on the stomach, and the baby shot out through the hands of the doctor and landed on the floor. The doctor picked up the baby nervously and accidentally hit the baby's head on the edge of the table. There was a hole in the baby's head and terrible brain damage had occurred.

The man later told me, "I was in that delivery room — saved, sanctified and filled with the Holy Ghost — but when I saw what the doctor did to my baby, I wanted to kill her."

It took a lot for him to confess that. It shows that you never know what is in a person's heart. It doesn't matter how well you speak in tongues. There is only one step from the spiritual to the carnal. This man had murder in his heart. He wanted to kill the doctor for hurting his baby.

But the young father's story doesn't end with a heart full of murder. Jesus appeared to him in that room and said, "Son, I can't do anything for you if you act like this."

When the young man told me this, he said, "Praise God, He still called me 'son,' even when I had murder in my heart!"

In other words, when you are in the carnal, God can't do anything for you. So, do you know what this man did? He walked right up to the doctor and said, "Please forgive me for talking to you like that. I am so sorry. Jesus just told me He is going to heal my baby."

The doctor, full of despair, replied, "Oh, your baby is going to die."

But the man said, "Oh no, my baby isn't going to die. Jesus said He is going to heal him."

She said, "If your baby lives, he will be a human vegetable. He won't be able to talk."

But the couple took that baby home. The father went to the bank and borrowed money for plane tickets to fly from Pittsburgh to Atlanta where we were holding meetings. They brought their baby to the crusade. The poor little guy had a plastic tube draining fluid off his brain. They unhooked his pajamas and showed me the spine outside his body, with some kind of plastic flesh sprayed over it by the doctors. I had never seen anything like it. The baby had spina bifida. His little toes were turned upward into his legs making his feet look like clubs.

I put that baby in my hands before I preached, and walked across that platform for about twenty minutes. I felt the anointing of God like I have never felt it before. In my spirit I knew God had healed that baby. Still, there was no evident sign. It takes faith to believe God when you can't see the signs.

I say this to encourage you. If you don't see immediate results, don't panic. Hold on to God's Word.

There was no immediate result. I put the baby back in his father's hands and said, "God has healed your baby! Take him home." The man didn't shout. In fact, he looked confused because the baby didn't look any different.

They took the baby back to the hospital. The doctor was there when the father checked the baby in. "You shouldn't have taken this baby out of the hospital," the doctor said. "He is worse!"

"That is what I thought," the man said, "but the preacher told me the baby is healed!"

The doctor said, "He must be a crazy preacher!"

But you see, the Bible says this is foolishness to the natural man. The natural man can't receive anything from God. It is foolishness to him.

So the downhearted father left the baby in the hospital and went back to work in the coal mines. As he picked up his pick and shovel, Jesus came into the coal mine. He looked directly at him, and said, "Son, why are you doubting Me? I have healed your baby."

The pick went one way and the shovel went another. He ran out of the mine, got on the telephone and called his wife. "Honey, get dressed! We are going to the hospital to get our baby. Jesus just stopped by the coal mine and told me He healed him!"

"I know it!" his wife replied. "Before He came to the mine, He came to me and told me the same thing!"

They went to the hospital and the father said to the doctor, "Get my baby ready! He is healed! I am taking him home!"

The doctor said, "Have you been talking to that crazy preacher again?"

"No!" the father answered. "I have been talking to the Man this time. When you get it from headquarters, you are healed!"

The baby wasn't healed right away. The court ordered those parents to take the baby to the Pittsburgh children's hospital. But this too was God's plan because this case is on record there. Sixteen doctors looked at that baby. While the greatest specialists on spina bifida checked that baby, God pushed the spine back into the baby's body and reduced the fluid in his head.

Later, I was preaching in Rex Humbard's church in Akron, Ohio. Sitting on the front row were the baby's parents with their baby boy. The proud father was waving happily at me, saying, "Hallelujah!"

The doctors had said the baby would be a vegetable, but he was healed by the power of the living Christ!

7

Child's Mind Healed

One day in New York, the Holy Ghost directed me to have a children's blessing service. A couple of days beforehand, a woman came to me and said, "Brother Schambach, I have a retarded son. When he was born, the doctors used instruments that damaged his head. It became odd shaped. After hearing you preach for a week, my faith has come alive. My son can't read or write. I believe that when you lay hands on him, God will perform a miracle, and he will be able to read and write."

I said, "Do you believe that?"

She said, "I believe it."

Children's blessing night came around, and I prayed for 3,000 children — right on Broadway in New York. I never saw so many kids in my life. I didn't know the woman's child from any other child, but I laid hands on each one.

That was on a Friday night. On Monday, the woman came back, and I knew something had happened. The ushers were trying to get her to keep quiet and stay in her seat, but I said, "Don't try to get her to sit down. God did something for her and I want to hear about it."

She came up and told the folks what God had done for her son, "I always got calls from his school teacher telling me he was a hyperactive child. He was always trouble. Monday morning I got another call from his teacher and I said, 'Oh no. What did he do now?' The teacher said, 'Oh, no, no, no, this is a good call. Something happened and we want to know what it is.' I said, 'What are you talking about? What happened to my boy?' She said, 'We don't know. That is why we are calling you. You know that your son can't read or write. Today I gave a test to my students. He picked up a pencil and did the test. I corrected the papers and he got 100 percent.'"

Now can you imagine? Put yourself in that teacher's shoes. If that was your pupil, and you saw 100 percent on a test from a child you knew couldn't read or write, what would you do?

The teacher said, "Sit down, boy. You are going to take this test again at my desk." He got 100 percent again! She was so overwhelmed that she took him to the principal's office. The principal gave him a third test, and he got his third 100 percent score.

The boy got more 100 percent marks in that one day than I got in my lifetime. The teacher said, "We want to know where you took him over the weekend."

The mother said, "I had him at a Holy Ghost revival, and the man of God laid hands on my son!"

She brought her boy with her to the service and showed him off to the crowd. "Look at this beautiful head," she said. "God even changed the shape of his head."

God will honor your faith. He will do what you believe Him for. That woman believed God could do it. I agreed with her. If two can agree as touching anything, it is done.

Six years later, that family became members of my church. The young lad graduated from high school with honors — a boy who couldn't read or write before.

8

The Poisoned Pie Lady

I preached on Broadway in New York City for fourteen solid weeks. The Holy Ghost came to Broadway. While I was there, an entire spiritualist church was set free. I cast the devil out of two of the church's members. They went back to their congregation and brought eight other members to my meetings. I cast the devil out of them, and they went and got twenty-four more. Finally, the whole spiritualist church was delivered. They had been workers of witchcraft.

One day I was walking out of the theater where the meetings were being held and a woman walked up to me and said, "I hate you!"

"Oh," I said, "I recognize your voice, you devil. I hate you too." I wasn't talking to the woman. I was talking to the devil in the woman.

She looked at me and said, "You ruined me!"

I said, "I don't even know you."

She said, "I had my people in the palm of my hand, and you set them free. My name is —, " she called herself Madam So-and-so.

I said, "Come here, madam. I will cast the devil out of you!"

She backed up. "Don't touch me!" she shrieked. "I have been watching you. The people in your meetings have been bringing you pies and cakes."

I said, "Yeah, and I am eating it all."

She said, "Preacher, I am going to fix you. I am going to bake a poisoned pie and hide it among them."

I said, "Do me a favor and make it coconut custard. Before I eat anything, I sanctify it! I have the power of the Holy Ghost inside of me!"

The woman was too flustered to say another word. She didn't have to. She had lost! Mark 16:18 says, . . . **and if they drink any deadly thing, it shall not hurt them.** . . .

I am talking about Holy Ghost power!

9

Man Spared From Electric Chair

This is one of the greatest miracles I have ever witnessed. I was preaching in Newark, New Jersey, in 1960. It is so vivid, I remember the time: 9:30. A woman came walking down the center aisle. I knew what that meant. It meant, "I am going to disturb you, preacher." She walked down that center aisle and stood right in front of me. I had my Bible in my hand, I was preaching — I was preaching a masterpiece! She interrupted me. How dare anybody interrupt a man of God?

Actually, I would hope more preachers were interrupted by someone with faith. Four men stopped Jesus when they tore the roof off and lowered down a man on a cot. They stopped Him from preaching. Remember what happened to the man on the cot?

When that woman came down and stopped me, she said, "Brother Schambach, please forgive me. I have never stopped a preacher in my life. But this is an emergency. My son is going to die in the electric chair at ten o'clock."

I said, "Oh, my God!" She knocked the preaching right out of me. I couldn't preach another word.

I had prayed for people dying in hospitals, but I had never prayed for anybody who was going to die in the electric chair. This man had been convicted by a jury of his peers. He had been found guilty. He was going to die in order to pay for the murder that they said he committed — and it was going to happen in thirty minutes. I couldn't preach! I shut the book. I couldn't even pray! I had everybody in that church stand.

People ask me, "Do I need the Holy Ghost?" I don't know about you, but I do. Sometimes I don't know how to pray. When I don't know how to pray, I let the Holy Ghost do the praying.

The Holy Ghost began to pray through me. I felt like somebody just put a robe on me. I could feel the anointing. A double portion came on me. I was praying in tongues. I wanted to eavesdrop on what the Holy Ghost was saying. How can you eavesdrop? Pray in English. So I stopped. When you are praying in the Spirit, your understanding is unfruitful. I didn't know what I was saying. Then all of a sudden, the understanding began to speak and the spirit was unfruitful. I began to pray in English, and what I was saying shocked me.

I will never forget my prayer. I was saying, "Lord, in the name of Jesus, convict the real killer through the Holy Ghost. Make him confess to the crime." Inside, I was kicking myself. I thought, "Shut up, dummy. The man has already been convicted." I was asking God to get a hold of the real killer. I didn't know, but the Holy Ghost knew that this woman's son hadn't committed the crime. The Holy Ghost was praying through me and saying, "Get a hold of the real killer and make him confess."

After I finished praying, I looked at that woman and said, "Go home, go to bed — and sleep! Your son will not die in the electric chair!" I could have kicked myself. I thought, *Shut up, you dumb preacher! Remember, you have to come back here tomorrow night and preach!*

Sometimes the Holy Ghost will say things that are difficult for you to believe. Sometimes when you are preaching, you say things that startle you. But it isn't you talking, it is the Holy Ghost.

Are you ready for the outcome of this story?

I returned to my hotel and went to bed. I got up the next morning and went to the diner a block away. On my way in, I bought the *New York Daily News*. Glory! Did you ever shout looking at a newspaper? Well, I did. You know what the headlines said? "Man's Life Spared From Electric Chair — Story on page 3." I didn't eat breakfast. Oh, no. I sat down on that curb and tore open the paper to page three. I can tell you what that newspaper said verbatim. I can tell you the name of the district attorney. His name was Mr. Hogan. The story said, "Last night at 9:40, Mr. Hogan received a phone call from a man." (Remember, it was 9:30 when the woman disturbed me. At 9:40, God answered the woman's prayer. Oh, hallelujah!) The man on the other end said, "You are burning the wrong man."

"What do you mean? Who is this?" asked Mr. Hogan.

"Never mind who it is. But you have a man scheduled to die in the electric chair for the murder of a man in the upper Bronx. You found his body in a second floor apartment, face down with stab wounds."

Mr. Hogan said, "How do you know this?"

He said, "I am the one who committed the crime."

"Where are you?" Mr. Hogan asked.

He answered, "I am two blocks from a certain precinct. And I am on my way in to give myself up."

Mr. Hogan stopped the execution. He went to the precinct and interrogated the new suspect until three o'clock in the morning, going over the same question. "Why did you give yourself up?"

Repeatedly the same answer came, "Man, I never had any intentions of giving myself up. But when I called you last night something got a hold of me and made me confess."

10
Seventeen Deaf Mutes Healed

In Africa, in a church with a crowd of 6,000 people, I suddenly stopped preaching. In the back there was a man sitting in the aisle, talking with his hands. I knew he was interpreting for the deaf. The anointing of God came on me. I stopped and said, "Brother, you back there in that aisle, you are disturbing me." He wasn't saying anything vocally, but he was conveying my message to people who couldn't hear. I wanted to capture his attention. And you know I did when I said that. I continued, "Brother, I am getting tired of you talking while I am talking. Bring all those deaf folks up here. God is going to heal them now."

Seventeen of them got up. Seventeen deaf mutes in Africa. I lined them up on the platform facing the people. Cameras were on. We were on television. The pastor of the church was nervously sitting on the edge of his chair.

I looked at the deaf people and saw one boy smiling from ear to ear.

"Yeah," I said to myself, "he's expecting something."

I had been preaching that Jesus Christ is the same today as He was yesterday. Well, if you believe that, demonstrate it. Paul said:

> And I, brethren, when I came to you, came not with excellency of speech or of wisdom, declaring unto you the testimony of God. And my speech and my preaching was not with enticing words of man's wisdom, but in demonstration of the Spirit and of power: That your

faith should not stand in the wisdom of men, but in the power of God.

1 Corinthians 2:1,4,5

I believe in what I preach. So I began to talk to that boy. I don't know sign language, so the man started to interpret. I said, "I don't need you anymore. Go sit down."

I put my finger in the boy's ears and in the name of Jesus took authority over that deaf and dumb spirit. I felt the spirit slide right by my finger. I knew he had come out — I knew it! I knew the boy's ears had opened. I spent about ten minutes with the lad and started teaching him English.

The pastor of the church was so blessed, he did a somersault in mid-air — and he was not an acrobat!

I went down the line. I got a hold of a woman, cast that spirit out of her and taught her to speak. I said to the pastor, "Bring the rest of your pastors here." There were thirty-five of them. I said, "Line them up. I am not going to wear myself out. Let them wear themselves out. Tell them to put their fingers in the people's ears. Tell them to put a thumb on their tongues. I will pray one prayer and God will heal all fifteen of them."

I prayed one prayer, talked to that deaf and dumb spirit, and in the name of Jesus commanded it to come out. The pastor took the microphone on television and went down the line. Each one heard and spoke!

11
Devils Recognize R.W.

I will never forget the first devil I cast out. I was with Brother A.A. Allen in Los Angeles. He cast the devils out of a girl who came to our meeting. We then moved to Phoenix and when I saw her walk inside the tent, I said, "Oh, Lord, they are all back, plus another thousand."

When Brother Allen saw her, he said, "Do you see what I see?"

I said, "Yes, sir."

"Oh," he said, "I can't tackle them tonight. If I pray for the sick, I won't be able to deliver her also. Take her in the prayer tent and cast them out."

I said, "What? You are the preacher."

He said, "I won't have anybody working with me who doesn't know how to cast out devils."

This was "where the rubber met the road." This was the nitty gritty now. This wasn't just playing church. I went to the platform and asked twelve of the pastors to come with me."

They said, "Where are we going?"

I said, "To battle. We are going to the prayer tent to battle." I picked six women with husky voices. I said, "Get the Blood songs ready. Just sing Blood songs. We are going to conquer the devil."

I was there from ten o'clock at night until one o'clock in the morning wrestling with those demons. I wrestled with the devils. It felt as though I had lost thirty pounds casting those demons out.

> **For we wrestle not against flesh and blood, but against principalities, against powers, against the rulers of the darkness of this world, against spiritual wickedness in high places.**
>
> **Ephesians 6:12**

I said, "Devil, in the name of Jesus, you are coming out."

The devil answered me back and said, "We are not coming out."

It wasn't just "I am not" but "we are not."

I wanted to say, "Go ahead, fella, stay where you are. I am not going to bother you."

But we ganged up on them. I quoted every Scripture passage I knew. I found out you can't beat the chair and pound them out. You can't stomp them out. You can't knock them out. You can't Scripture-quote them out. You have to cast them out. This is what God told us to do. Finally, at three o'clock in the morning, the devil said, "We are going to wear you out."

He didn't know how close to the truth he was. I said, "Devil, we don't wear out." I felt like somebody put a mantle on me. I said, "Satan, my elder brother Jesus destroyed you 2,000 years ago." The moment I said it, the voice inside that woman said, "Don't say that."

I said, "I got him. I got him!" So, being an obedient servant, I shouted it again. I learned my lesson a long time ago. When the devil tells you not to do something, do it. And when he tells you to do something, don't do it.

I said, "He has his bags packed. He is on his way." I shouted it louder one more time.

The devil said, "I know it. But don't say it so loud. Everybody doesn't know it."

When Jesus died on Calvary and shed His blood, He paid the price. I believe the devils came out of everybody so they could gather around the cross of Calvary and wring their hands and say, "We got Him now."

But they didn't have Him! Jesus died on the cross, defeating sin and Satan. No one destroyed the kingdom of the devil like Jesus did!

> **I am he that liveth, and was dead; and, behold, I am alive for evermore, Amen; and have the keys of hell and of death.**
>
> **Revelation 1:18**

Those devils finally came out of that woman. I made sure that she received Christ into her heart and was baptized in the Holy Ghost. When we heard her speaking in other tongues, we knew those devils would never return again. Praise God!

> **Ye are of God, little children, and have overcome them: because greater is he that is in you, than he that is in the world.**
>
> **1 John 4:4**

12

The Baby With the Rubber Legs

At one of my meetings I saw an elderly lady with a baby. I knew it wasn't hers. I walked over to her and said, "Mother, this isn't your baby, is it?"

She said, "No, I am the grandmother. It is my son's baby. This child is six years old. He has never had a haircut; he has no teeth; and he has never walked." There didn't seem to be a joint in the knee. His legs were like rubber.

I asked where the father was.

"Oh," she said, "he doesn't believe in this. My son and his wife go to bars at night."

I said, "We are not going to pray for him tonight. Take him home and dump him in your son's lap. Tell him that if he wants the baby healed, he needs to bring him here."

Pretty hard, isn't it? But I don't preach crusades to win a popularity contest. I come to preach the Word. That woman understood it. She said, "I will do it, Brother Schambach."

The following night, I saw them sitting towards the front. As I walked in, I saw the mother nudge her son and say, "That is him." A grouchy look came over his face. He was mad because I made him come to church. He was missing one of his beer-drinking nights.

I came up to him and said, "Are you the daddy? Do you want to see your son healed?"

He said, "What kind of father do you think I am?"

I said, "I am about to find out. Look at me, mister. That baby was born under a curse. If you want that curse to be lifted, get on your knees right now and give your life to Jesus. You aren't going to wait for an altar call. You need to get saved now. I am going to find out what kind of a father you are."

The man turned in his seat and made an altar out of it. He cried out to God. I said to the lady next to him, "Are you his wife? Do you want your baby healed?"

She said, "I sure do."

I told her, "Kneel by your husband and give your life to Jesus."

Both gave their lives to Christ that night. When the man of God laid hands on him, the child took his first step. We put him on the platform and although he had never walked in his six years of life, he took his first steps that night.

This family became very close to me. They loved me because I had told them the truth. I received a letter from the father six months after the crusade. It said, "My son has had six haircuts. He has a full set of teeth. He is growing and talking. Thank God you told us the truth. A curse has been lifted and now the blessing is mine." Hallelujah!

13
Mama Helps Break
Son Out of Prison

One day, while preaching in Ashland, Virginia, I was on my way to the main auditorium. Suddenly, a six-foot five-inch black man jumped out from a tree and grabbed me. I was in his grip and I couldn't get out. He asked, "Are you Schambach?"

For the first time in my life, I didn't know whether to tell the truth. So being the politician I am, I asked, "Why?"

He said, "If you are him, you helped get me saved."

I said, "I am him, brother."

He told me one of the most beautiful stories. He said, "Brother Schambach, I had two life sentences hanging on my neck. I wasn't eligible for parole for another ten years. My mama stood in a proxy line in your tent. I was a black Muslim. I hated preachers, particularly white preachers. My mama came into your proxy service and stood for me."

He told me he was in the middle of a hold-up when his mama stood in that line. But he said, "Thank God, the cops got me and arrested me. If they hadn't, I would have died and gone to hell. While in prison my mama gave me a Bible. I tore it up and flushed it down the commode. I hated anything that had the word "Christian" on it. She sent me a radio. When you are in prison, you will listen to anything. I used to listen to that Nashville sound, but then a preacher by the name of Schambach came on. I thought he was black.

I used to listen to you on the radio. You made me so mad that once I jumped up and down on that radio and broke it. My mama sent me another radio."

Isn't that just like a mother? Mamas don't give up.

He said, "There I was in that cell. When you are in a cell and have nowhere to go, you will listen to anything. I listened to you every single night. God started mellowing my heart. I fell on my face and repented of my sin. God saved me and filled me with the Holy Ghost. I wrote to your office and you sent me literature and a Bible. I started having Bible studies right there in the prison."

A revival broke out. Convicts got saved and filled with the Holy Ghost. A guard came to this same man and said, "The parole board wants to see you."

He said, "Oh, not me. I am not eligible for parole for at least ten more years."

"That may be, but they are asking for you," the guard told him. "And not only the parole board, but the governor is there also."

He walked in and the governor asked, "What are you doing in this prison?"

He answered, "Serving time."

The governor said, "Other than that, what you are doing is rehabilitating prisoners."

The young man said, "Not me, sir. Jesus is doing that."

The governor said, "Well, whatever. I have a full pardon for you. The government gives us hundreds of thousands of dollars for rehabilitation and we can't do a thing with prisoners. You aren't getting a dime and you are rehabilitating them. So I am going to give you a full pardon."

The young man said, "Governor, that is two pardons I have gotten in my life. Jesus gave me one and now you are giving me another."

The governor looked at him and said, "Yes, but this pardon is conditional. It has a string attached to it. You will have to return here twice a week and preach this Jesus until He comes."

Isn't that beautiful? Some of my friends who are businessmen went into that prison with him. A revival broke out. When the young man got his pardon, one of the businessmen, a Christian tailor, made him four brand-new suits.

By now, as the young black man concluded his story, I was practically shouting. He said, "Brother Schambach, this suit didn't cost me a dime. One of the businessmen you sent to the prison is a contractor and he gave me a job. The other is a builder of condominiums. He gave me a free apartment. I don't have to pay rent."

I looked at him and said, "Pick me up and let's dance one more time, brother!"

All this happened because that man had a mama who wouldn't give up on him. Don't give up. Don't give up. Don't give up!

14
Sharon's New Eye Miracle

My wife and I pastored a church in the early 1950s. A man, who later became a dear friend of mine, used to bring his six-year-old daughter to Sunday school. He would always drop her off and I would wonder who her parents were. But he would never come to Sunday school. He would never come to church.

One day I jumped in front of his car to stop him. I wanted to talk to him. But he knew who I was and that was the last time I jumped in front of his car. He put it in gear and laid the rubber down. I flew into the bushes. He didn't want to talk to a preacher.

I was after that big fish. I liked that little girl coming to Sunday school, but I wanted the father to come also. However, he couldn't bring himself to come to church. I knew he was a sinner. Sinners don't like to go to church.

One day my wife and I were on vacation visiting her mother in Philadelphia. I got a long-distance phone call. I heard a strange voice on the other end of the line. The man had tears in his voice. He said, "Brother Schambach?"

I said, "Who is this?" It was that little girl's father. I said, "Oh, something must be wrong. You called me brother. You tried to run over me last time we met. What is wrong?"

He said "I am in the hospital in McKeesport, Pennsylvania."

I said, "What is wrong with you?"

"Nothing is wrong with me. It is my daughter."

That daughter was the apple of her daddy's eye. "What happened?" I asked.

He told me that his family was visiting them. While the children were playing in the back yard, her cousin picked up a rusty nail and threw it. It was an accident, but it hit his daughter in the eye and shattered the eyeball. The doctors wanted to cut the eye out.

"Well," I said, "let them operate."

He said, "She told me to call you!"

I said, "What would you like me to do?" I wanted him to lay it on the line.

"She wants you to come and bring that bottle of oil. She says that if you pray for her, everything will be all right."

Kids have faith! "Well," I said, "I am thankful she wants me to come. I am her pastor. What about you?"

He said, "Please come."

I replied, "I am on my way. Don't let the doctors operate. Don't let them do anything until I get there." I took the next plane out.

I had visited that hospital practically every day in the past. Doctors there knew me on a first name basis. I would pray and minister to the sick. Two of the young interns met me at the entrance. They said, "Hurry up and do your thing. An infection is setting in the eye. We have to take her to the operating room and remove the eye."

I said, "Now, hold on, fellows. What makes you think that after I do my thing, you are going to have to do your thing? That is why I have been called. That girl is expecting a miracle!"

Children believe God. I would rather lay hands on a child than on an adult any day. It is the adults I have problems with. Children believe anything you tell them. The adults, however, deal with logic all the time. They want to know what makes it work. They want to logically figure it out. That is why adults often get nothing from God. A child just says, "Pray for me, I will be all right."

The interns said, "We aren't going to argue with you. Go in anyway."

I didn't go in the room. I headed for the waiting room because I knew her father would be there. I wasn't about to go in and pray for that girl. I wanted that man first. He wasn't going to run over me anymore.

There he was. He was weeping. His daughter was suffering.

I said, "I finally caught up with you. Get on your knees. It is time to pray now."

The two doctors came in and said, "Will you please come with us? The trouble isn't here, it is inside."

I answered, "That is why you are a doctor and not a preacher. You don't even know where the trouble is. I have been after this guy for about nine months. I am not about to let this fish go now. Get on your knees, brother. We are getting right with God."

I didn't have to beg him. He fell on his face. He prayed and we touched God. God saved him and gave him a miracle in his life. After God transformed him, I said, "Let's go now." We headed for Sharon's room. I will never forget her. She was a pretty little blond girl. There she was, lying on her bed with a patch over her eye. When I stepped in, she turned to me and smiled. "I knew you would come," she said softly. "Everything is all right now."

I got out my bottle of oil and walked towards her. There were two doctors standing next to me. They said, "What are you doing?" I got my bottle out and put oil on her. They were looking at the oil and saying, "Can I look at that? What is this, holy oil?"

I said, "No. I got it from my wife's kitchen. She fries chicken in it. I bought it at the A&P. There isn't anything holy about the oil. Oil can't heal you. You can go swim in oil and it won't heal you."

And the prayer of faith shall save the sick, and the Lord shall raise him up; and if he have committed sins, they shall be forgiven him.

James 5:15

There is something about a child who just believes God. I didn't want to answer all those questions, so I said to the doctors, "Please wait outside, will you? Wait until I get done. You don't let me in your operating room, so please step out of mine."

They went out. I didn't even bother to look at the eye. I didn't have to look at it — I wasn't a doctor. I laid hands on her and said a simple prayer. I didn't even shake. I said, "Father, in the name of Jesus, perform the miracle and give her a new eye." That is all I said. I turned to the door and saw the two doctors. I waved for them to come in.

They asked, "Can we have her now, Reverend?" They were getting testy with me now. They had never called me Reverend before.

I said, "What are you going to do with her?"

"Well, we told you the eye is infected. We have to cut it out."

I said, "It isn't infected anymore."

"What are you talking about?"

I said, "Didn't you tell me that the eye was shattered in a hundred pieces? You said that. I never even looked at it."

"Why, of course, that is why we have to operate."

I said, "You don't have to take her anymore. God just performed a miracle." I knew that little girl had faith. I knew God wasn't going to disappoint that faith. He never disappoints faith.

They said, "What do you mean?"

I said, "Look at the eye."

They went over, took the bandage off and took a peek at it.

"I don't believe it," the doctors exclaimed.

I said, "That is the reason I had you stand outside the door. You can't believe it even when you look at it."

Jesus said,

And blessed is she that believed: for there shall be a performance of those things which were told her from the Lord.

Luke 1:45

God is looking for men and women who will stand on His Word believing that if He said it, He will do it, and that if He spoke it, He will bring it to pass. God has to take you outside that human realm in order to do something supernatural.

15

Brother Leroy Gets Saved

In 1956 I was called back from the evangelistic field to bury my mama.

All of us remaining six kids were at her bedside when she died. She wasn't asking God to give her more life. My mother lived a full life. She had raised twelve kids. Six of us were left. Do you know what Mama was doing? She was crying out to God. She said, "Oh God, You promised me You would save all my children." Her dying cry was for her kids.

All of us were saved and filled with the Holy Ghost except my younger brother Leroy. He was six foot four inches and 240 pounds of solid steel. He was standing next to me at our dying mother's bedside. I gave him a poke in the ribs — almost broke my elbow.

I said, "Come on, boy. Get right with God before Mom goes."

He said, "Hey, not now. Mama is dying." He loved Mom just as much as anybody, but he was a backslider.

We buried Mom. She died without seeing that answer. Does that mean God isn't faithful? Of course not. I went back to the evangelistic field. I was traveling with Brother Allen at the time. We were in California. I had a great burden for my brother. It hit me all of a sudden, when Brother Allen was giving an altar call. I leaped off that platform. I jumped in the altar call for salvation.

Brother Allen said, "What are you doing there Schambach? The call is for sinners. It doesn't look good that my afternoon speaker is getting saved."

We are always making judgments on others, aren't we? We don't know what is going on in a person's heart. But I stayed there and said, "Lord, I am no longer R.W., I am Leroy. If he isn't going to get saved, I am going to get saved for him." Now, I had never heard anybody say that before, but I felt that. I wanted to get saved for him. I went into that prayer tent. I got on my face. I cried out to God.

The next day I had a call from my sister Margaret. I said, "Margaret, am I ever glad you called. I have some good news for you."

She said, "Will you let me talk? I am paying for this call."

I said, "You can talk when I get done. I have some good news. Leroy is saved!"

There was a silence on the phone.

I said, "Margaret, did you hear what I said?"

She said, "How did you know?"

I said, "How did I know? You don't know what I went through last night, girl." I told her how I took his place and answered the altar call, crying out to God to have mercy.

She said, "That's what I called to tell you. Last night we were all in church. All except Leroy. He was out living it up, having a ball. Halfway through the sermon, Leroy walked in. He didn't even stop to sit in a pew. He headed for the altar. He draped his six foot four frame over the altar and cried out to God. God saved him and filled him with the Holy Ghost."

Leroy didn't hear a sermon. Sometimes we preachers think we preach masterpieces. But people aren't getting saved because of the preaching. It is the Holy Ghost who takes them to the cross.

It works!

16
Spinal Meningitis Miracle

I was preaching in Buffalo, New York, when a gentleman invited me and my staff to his home for dinner. We enjoy invitations like that when we can because we get tired of quarter-pounders and French fries. One thing he forgot to tell me, however, is that he didn't live in Buffalo. He lived in Niagara Falls.

My meetings don't get out at nine o'clock. When you lay hands on thousands of people, it gets close to the midnight hour. After the meeting, we had to travel all the way to Niagara Falls. Whenever I am invited out, I fast all day. I make sure I don't eat anything because I like to fill up while I am there.

The man's wife had outdone herself with the menu. It was one of the most bountiful tables I have ever seen. She had roast turkey, porterhouse steak, roast beef and fried chicken. (In that part of the country, you don't invite a preacher unless you have fried chicken.) The gentleman asked me to pray. I blessed the food.

We were anxious to start eating, but when the man began to speak, what he had to say was more interesting than the food. I actually pushed my plate back to listen.

He said he had never been sick a day in his life. He had money in the bank. His future was secure. He worked for the government. But all of a sudden something struck him — spinal meningitis — and paralyzed him from head to toe. He spent over three months in the hospital. Doctors were called in from all over the world. His bank account dwindled. He had to sell his home for the equity to pay the doctor bills. Rheumatoid arthritis crept into every joint until he couldn't stand the pain. He lapsed into a coma for almost four months.

Since the man was Roman Catholic, his priest was called to administer the last rites of that church. Lying in the coma, he knew what the priest was doing, but he couldn't communicate because he was paralyzed. "I couldn't flicker an eyelash," he recalled. How would you feel when you know that the priest is giving you the last rites — the last ceremony in the Catholic church before you die?

As soon as the priest left, *another priest* walked through the wall and over to the bed. There was something different about this priest. He was dressed all in white. The new priest leaned down to the dying man and called him by name. He said, "You don't have any trouble. All you need is faith in God."

Of course, the man was laying there thinking, "What kind of crazy priest is this? I don't have any trouble? Here I am in a coma. I can't communicate. There is arthritis in every joint, I have spinal meningitis. I had to sell my home. My bank account is gone. Is this not trouble?

But the priest said, "I am Jesus of Nazareth, and I am going to heal you right now."

Isn't that beautiful. Jesus said, "When I walk out of this room, I want you to get out of this bed. Shave, wash and walk out of this hospital. Go to the first bookstore you can find and buy a Bible. Start reading from St. John's gospel. You will find the way to eternal life."

Oh, hallelujah! The man told us that Jesus turned and walked right back through the wall. As the man was telling me this story, he looked at me and said, "Brother Schambach, I wonder why Jesus didn't just use the door."

I said, "He is the door!"

He can make an entrance wherever you are. He can come right into your automobile. He can visit you on your job. He can walk into your bedroom. No matter where you are, Jesus is the door. He will come in!

When Jesus walked out of that room, the man got out of bed and started shaving. The nurse came tip-toeing in. She wanted to pull the sheet over because the other priest had walked out. But she saw the bed empty. She ran into the bathroom and said, "Please get back into bed. Don't you know you are dying? The priest gave you the last rites."

The man said to her, "Cool it, honey. Another priest came in and gave me the 'first rites' all over again. I am going to live!"

When you have an experience with God, you are never at the mercy of a man with an argument. People will come to you and say, "I don't believe in healing." All you have to do is laugh and say, "Then you can stay sick. But my God healed me."

17

R.W.'s High School Bully

When I was in high school I was just a little fellow — six foot tall, 160 pounds. The reason I felt little is that there was a big guy in my class who was six foot six inches. He weighed about 270 pounds. He liked me. He liked me so well he used to beat me every day. He would slap my head. I would turn around and say, "I bumped into your hand. Pardon me." I wasn't about to tangle with him.

When he saw me coming down the hall with my books, he would knock the books out of my hand and trip me. I would get up and apologize for running into his foot. He zeroed in on me. All through the ninth, tenth and eleventh grades, I took it. My shins were black and blue. I wore out three sets of books, and not from studying. As long as I was willing to take it, he dished it out.

One day I was home by myself. All the other kids had gone somewhere with Mom. I was alone in the house, in the bathroom, naked to the waist, looking in the mirror. When we are young, we stand in front of the mirror and flex our muscles. I would look in the mirror and say, "Charles Atlas!" Then I would say, "Yeah! There isn't anybody who can beat you! Yeah! Next time that giant slaps you alongside the head, you turn around and challenge him. Yeah!"

Of course, he wasn't around. But I was psyched up. A mirror will do wonders for you.

The next morning I went through the door to the school's long hallway. There were no exits. As soon as I came in, I saw him coming the other way. I walked the length of that corridor with my eyes on the giant. My heart was doing a flip. Something inside said, "Remember last night in the mirror."

I thought, "Shut up in there." I had lost the momentum.

He got about fifty feet from me. . .then thirty, twenty, and my eyes were still in this direction. Before long he got close and then went by. Finally I breathed. Whew!

But just when I thought I was out of danger, somehow he sneaked up behind me and slapped me alongside my head one more time. Before I knew what I was doing, I turned around and dropped my books and said, "Hold it!"

He turned around with a silly looking grin on his face. He laid his books down. He said, "I have been waiting three years for you."

I looked at him and pointed my finger and for a few seconds said nothing. I was frozen. I couldn't speak. I stood shaking, until it finally came out, "You have hit me for the last time."

He came at me and I dug into that linoleum. I had made up my mind I wasn't running anymore. I had had it. I was fed up with it. I was tired of it. I wasn't going to get black and blue anymore. I didn't have the money to buy any more new books. I said, "You and I are going at it, mister!"

It was only two hits. I hit him and he hit the floor. I knocked him out. You talk about getting happy. I called all my buddies to see what I had done. . ."Look! Look! I did it!"

Then I got mad. I thought, "All these years he had me buffaloed. I didn't know he had a glass jaw. If I would have done this three years ago, I would have saved myself all that mess."

Don't bother to judge me about this incident, because I wasn't saved then. I was a little devil then. But when I got saved, God brought that event back to my mind to let me know that this is what Jesus did to the devil 2,000 years ago. You and I don't have to be afraid of the devil, because he has a glass jaw, and Jesus has already knocked him out!

18

Miracle Candy

I don't only pray over cloths, I also wear the cloths. Paul took cloths and aprons from his body and sent them to the sick, the diseased, the afflicted and the demon possessed. The Bible says he took them off of his body. He must have had them on his body at some point. When you preach under the anointing of the Holy Ghost, it penetrates everything you have on. It isn't the cloth that heals. If cloth healed, you wouldn't be sick. It is what is behind that cloth — the faith of that individual — that produces the healing.

One night in Philadelphia, a lady came to me and gave me some candy to wear. You can tell by looking at me that I like candy. So I accepted it and thanked her for it. She said, "That isn't for you."

"Well," I said, "you just gave it to me."

She said, "I want you to wear it."

I said, "Hold it, girl. I don't wear candy. I eat candy. What is wrong with you?"

She said, "Now, Brother Schambach, you are going to wear that candy while you preach."

Did you ever run into a stubborn woman? There are a lot of women who will never take no for an answer — they are going to press through and get what God has promised them. This was one of those ladies. She said, "You are going to wear that candy."

I said, "No, I am not going to wear it, woman. What is wrong with you? Other preachers already talk about me wearing cloth. If they find out I am wearing candy, my name is mud."

She said, "Brother 'Mud,' you are going to wear that candy."

She was very persistent. I said, "I am not going to wear it." I just withdrew myself from it. I said, "Why don't you make it a cloth like everybody else does? I will give you a cloth — take my hanky!"

"No, I don't want it," she said. "You are going to wear this candy. I have cloths from your office. I have them from Oral Roberts. I have them from T.L. Osborn. I have a sister in a mental institution. She has been there for thirty years. I send her those cloths, but they censor her mail and they know what those cloths are. The cloths end up in the wastebasket. I just came from there and they told me I can send candy to my sister. Now, you and I are going to put one over on the devil. We are going to cast him out with that candy."

I looked at her and said, "Give me the candy!" I put it in my left hip pocket and started preaching. I returned it to her at the end of the service. "You send it to your sister," I told her.

Six months later, I came back to that city, and I was preaching in the Metropolitan Opera House. I was receiving the offering that night when I saw two ladies come in. To be perfectly honest with you, I didn't remember the woman with the candy. She came walking down the aisle and dropped her offering in the basket and said, "Praise the Lord, Brother Schambach."

I said, "Praise the Lord."

She said, "This is my sister."

I said, "Hi sister, glad to have you in church."

She said, "Brother Schambach, I said this is my sister."

So I dropped the bucket, got her by the hand and said, "Welcome to our crusade." I didn't want to offend her.

She said, "Brother Schambach, do you remember who I am?"

I said, "No, ma'am, I am sorry I don't."

She said, "I am the one who gave you the candy!"

I stopped the offering collection and said, "Everybody go sit down. Forget the offering. I want to hear this."

I didn't get to preach that night. That woman tore the place apart. She told the story that I just told you. Then she said, "I sent that candy to the hospital, and the moment my sister bit into the candy, she bit into the power of God. The demons came out of her instantly and she was in her right mind for the first time in thirty years."

The hospital staff didn't call the sister for about two weeks. Can you imagine that telephone call? "Come and get your sister."

"What do you mean, come and get her. Is she dead?"

"No! She isn't dead!"

"Well, what is wrong?"

"We don't know. All we know is that for the last two weeks, we have put her through a series of tests. She has been examined by every psychiatrist and every psychologist who had anything to do with her case. For the first time in thirty years, your sister is in her right mind."

What a miracle! This woman started attending a church in Philadelphia that used to be pastored by my brother-in-law, Rev. Harry Donald. She went on to live a normal life and was able to work because her sister didn't give up!

But the preacher almost cost her the miracle. . ."I am not going to wear that candy!" I learned my lesson that night!

19
Death of a Rebellious Teenager

When my wife and I finished school in 1950, we pastored a church in Glassport, Pennsylvania, a suburb of Pittsburgh. There was a young woman in that church who had lost her mother and father. She had a brother, sixteen years of age, for whom she was responsible.

I fasted and prayed for that boy. I had all-night prayer meetings. I fasted weeks at a time for him. One night, he came to church. He had a helmet in his hand. He belonged to a black-jacketed motorcycle gang.

His sister got him to come to church and I was elated. I said, "Oh, Holy Ghost, you have to save him tonight."

We had ordered pews to be made for our church. They were placed against the wall, so folks couldn't get out. I had them custom-designed that way. That evening, when I gave the altar call and people came to get saved, he just sat there, tears running down his face. While they were singing an invitational song, I went back and slid in — I knew he couldn't get out. I threw my arm around him. I cried with him and said, "Come on, son. I have been praying for you. I have fasted for you. Tonight is your night. Jesus wants to come into your life."

He said, "Oh, not tonight, preacher. I am a young man. I have my entire life ahead of me. I am only sixteen. I want to see what it's like to serve the devil, then I will come. Not tonight."

Then I got rough. I said, "Man, what is wrong with you? Who do you think you are? You don't have a guaranteed tomorrow. I don't care how old you are." I put my arm around him. He was weeping. The Holy Ghost was melting his heart, yet he rejected God.

For twenty minutes he evaded my grasp. "Not tonight, preacher. Some other time."

He walked out of the church. At 3:30 in the morning, a phone call got me out of bed. It was the young man's sister on the phone. She was weeping. "Brother Schambach, will you conduct my brother's funeral?"

I said, "Oh, no. I didn't know you had another brother."

She said, "I didn't. It is the one who was in church tonight."

No wonder I pleaded with him for twenty minutes. The Holy Ghost wouldn't let me turn him loose. I don't do that frequently. I tell folks, "If you want to go to hell, help yourself." But the Holy Ghost gave him twenty more minutes.

I asked what had happened.

He had a date with 300 of his motorcycle gang members to drive from the town of Elizabeth to Pittsburgh. His helmet was on, and the visor was down. Those bikes were going seventy miles an hour. I am sure the Holy Ghost was still dealing with him. Perhaps hot tears were coming out of his eyes. Perhaps he couldn't see where he was going. What we do know is he hit the median strip going 70 miles an hour into oncoming traffic. An eighteen-wheeler loaded with 85,000 pounds of steel was heading downhill. The motorcycle struck the radiator of the eighteen-wheeler and got buried in it.

The boy died instantly. I went to Duchane, Pennsylvania, to the funeral home. There were 300 kids smoking marijuana, waiting for the funeral. I got half-loaded just from walking through that crowd. I went inside, and the mortician met me. "Are you the preacher?"

I said, "Yes."

He said, "Hurry up and get it over with so I can put him in the ground. I don't want these kids hanging around."

I said, "Mind your own business. You are the undertaker. I am the man of God here. I came here to preach this funeral. I am not preaching to empty chairs. You can have the body, but I am going to preach to those kids. If they don't come in, I will preach to them on the sidewalk."

I went out on the sidewalk and introduced myself. "I am the pastor here. You have come to pay your respects to your buddy. Where do you want to do it, here on the street or inside?" They all followed me in.

I was fresh out of Bible school. I had never conducted a funeral before in my life. I didn't really know how.

Of course, the casket was closed because the body was so mangled. I took the flowers that were all over the casket and threw them off. I grabbed the casket and wheeled it right down in front of the kids. I slapped my hand on the top of that casket and said, "Here lies the remains of your buddy. If this young man didn't give his heart to the Lord after he left my meeting, then his soul is in hell." All those kids jumped up, angry. But I said, "This is one preacher who isn't going to lie to you. I won't lie and go to hell for anybody."

Many preachers lie over caskets every time they bury someone. Some dead people are so crooked they have to screw them into the ground — then we stand over them and say, "He was a wonderful man."

I looked at those kids and said, "I gave this young man seven hours of my life. I gave up about 21 meals for him. I fasted and prayed for him. I had all-night prayer meetings. I prayed for this boy. Last week, I cornered him, and he rejected God."

I gave an altar call, 150 of the 300 kids came and knelt around his casket and gave their lives to Jesus Christ.

Am I trying to tell you that boy had to die so that 150 people would get saved? No, that has already been done. I know somebody who died 2,000 years ago so that the whole world could be saved!

20
The Back Rent Blues

One night, at a crusade meeting, a lady walked down the aisle of the big auditorium. Tears were streaming down her face. She was holding a long sheet of paper.

There were 1,500 to 2,000 people in the audience, and everybody was being blessed but her. She was weeping desperately, grieving so deeply that it kind of grew over the whole congregation.

She said, "Brother Schambach, they are going to put me out of my house. I am four months behind in my rent." She held up the paper. "This is a notice of eviction. Tomorrow morning at 10 o'clock, they are going to move everything out to the sidewalk."

I jumped off that platform and said, "Woman, the devil is a liar. They are not putting you out on the sidewalk. You are a child of God."

She said, "What about this notice?"

I took it, tore it up and threw it under the platform. "That is your problem. You are looking at the circumstances. If you continue to do that, you will not have faith. You have to start looking in the Bible.

But God shall supply all your need according to his riches in glory by Christ Jesus.
Philippians 4:19

The reason sick people can't get healed is that they are too busy looking at their diseases. The more they look at them, the worse they feel. We need to keep our eyes on the Word.

I did my best to encourage this woman's faith. She was weeping vehemently.

She said, "Brother Schambach, my blind mama lives with me, and all I can see is my blind mother sitting on the step."

I said, "Shut up! You are getting to me now, woman!" (I guess that is why I am not pastoring anymore.) The devil is not going to put you out on the sidewalk. Sit down in that front row and listen to me preach."

I have never seen such anxiety in an individual. I had a sermon prepared but didn't use it. I left all those people, jumped down to where she was, and I preached to that woman for a solid hour. She needed it. I didn't even receive the offering until I finished preaching. Then, when I finished preaching, I went to her and said, "It is time to receive the offering."

She almost fainted. She looked up at me and said, "Don't you remember me? I need money."

I said, "I know it. Where is your pocketbook?"

She said, "But I need ——"

I knew she needed money. I am a good listener. She told me she was four months behind in the rent. She also said, "I gave the man $50 but he threw it back at me because it wasn't nearly enough." I had heard that part. I knew she had $50.

I asked, "Where is your purse?"

She said, "Mama has it." Her blind mother was in the service.

I said, "Get it. You are going to give something to God."

She got mad at me. You can tell when folks get mad. But I stayed sweet because I knew she was going to be glad all over again. I was showing her the way to deliverance, and she didn't know it. I said, "We don't have much time. It is ten o'clock at night. At ten o'clock in the morning, they are coming to evict you. You do what I tell you to do, woman."

I could have taken the money out of the church treasury, and I could have paid her rent. But then she would have owed it to God, because that is God's money.

I thought, "Why not just put your faith to work and let her receive a blessing? When God blesses her with it, she will have to pay the tithe and everyone will be blessed." This is how God works!

The woman got up in a huff and went to the back to get her purse. I saw her coming and turned my back to her as I was holding the bucket. I didn't know whether she was going to hit me with her purse or what. I didn't even want to see what she put in.

But I had challenged her to give, and she gave. When it came time for prayer, I said, "I want your blind mama first in that line." Her blind mother was indeed the first in line. I said to the woman, "Stand behind her." Then, I called the prayer line. I laid hands on 500 or 600 people that night, including the blind woman. I rebuked the blind spirit. Her eyes didn't come open suddenly. Sometimes God does it suddenly, instantly, immediately — but sometimes the healing is gradual. Yet in my spirit, I knew God had healed her.

I told her, "Mother, will you do what I tell you to do?"

She said, "Anything you say, I will do it." What a difference between her and her daughter.

I said, "Mama, I want you to go home tonight saying nothing but 'Thank You, Jesus, for giving me twenty-twenty vision.' Keep thanking Him till your head hits the pillow. You will wake up with perfect sight."

She said "I will do it." She started down the ramp and said, "Devil, you are a liar. I am not blind anymore. I am thanking Jesus for twenty-twenty vision."

I said, "Go ahead, Mama, the whole way home."

Then it was time to pray for the woman. I laid hands on her also. I prayed a very simple prayer. I said, "Lord, I don't know how You are going to do this." I don't know how He heals folks either. All I know is He does it. So I prayed, "I am asking You to perform a miracle and pay this woman's debt." Then I said to the woman, "Look at me. In the name of Jesus, I command you to go home and unpack all those bags."

She said, "How do you know I have my bags packed?"

I said, "The way you are talking, I am surprised you haven't moved."

She said, "Half of it is at my brother's house."

"Well, get it back," I answered. "You aren't going anywhere."

That was a Sunday night. On Monday night, I was getting ready to preach when the back door of the church bounced open. This woman wasn't walking in, she was floating in. She was six feet in the air! She was halfway down the aisle when I stopped her.

"Don't you remember me?" she asked.

I said, "I know who you are. But I am not passing up this opportunity for a sermon. I want to ask you one question. Why didn't you come to church like that last night?"

We let our troubles get to us.

I said, "The way you came into this building tonight is the way you ought to come to church no matter what kind of trouble you are going through. Psalm 100:4 says, **Enter into his gates with thanksgiving and into his courts with praise: be thankful unto him, and bless his name.** I can tell by looking at you that God did something. Come down here."

She said, "This morning, I was awakened by the smell of coffee brewing, bacon frying and homemade biscuits baking. I sat up in my bed, catching the aroma of this breakfast. I looked over into my blind mama's bed and it was empty. I quickly threw on a robe and ran out into the kitchen. There was my mama making breakfast. She has been blind for sixteen years, brother."

She said, "Mama, what are you doing?"

Her mother said, "Brother Schambach told me I would wake up seeing this morning and the man of God was right. You have been making my breakfast all these years — I thought I would give you the best breakfast you ever had, daughter."

The daughter said, "We didn't eat breakfast. We had church in the kitchen at eight o'clock in the morning. At ten o'clock the constable was supposed to be there. I looked up and said, 'Oh, God, if You can open Mama's eyes, You can pay the rent. Take Your time, You still have two hours.'"

That is what I call faith. I don't know whether I could have said that with only two hours left, but when God does something for you personally, you can trust Him for the next hurdle.

At 8:30 the mailman came. She thought, "Maybe this is the way God is going to do it." She picked up and opened the six letters she had received. You know how you open the mail looking for money? But there was no money — instead she got bills! Isn't that just like the devil? Now that her faith was strong and she was trusting God for money, she got four bills. But she just laid them on the table and said, "Lord, while You are paying the rent, please catch these four bills too!"

It was nine o'clock. The phone rang. It was a call from a woman whose name she didn't even remember.

"Well, you should remember me," the lady said. "Fourteen or fifteen years ago, you loaned me some money."

"Yeah! Now I remember you." But she never thought she would get that money back.

The lady said, "Honey, I know you thought I would never pay you back. But last night something got a hold of me." The woman explained that she had been in Chicago, shopping, when an overwhelming power took hold of her and seemed to push her towards State Street. She found herself at the Pacific Garden Mission, the famous ministry where Billy Sunday got saved. I have visited that place many times. It is still open and many people get saved in that mission. But this lady had never been to a mission in her life. The Holy Ghost dragged her in, and she sat in the back seat. A man stood up behind the rostrum to give his sermon. At the close, he gave an altar call. The lady got up. The same power that had dragged her down State Street also dragged her down that aisle. She was on her knees getting saved at the altar.

This is the best part of the story as far as I am concerned. That woman not only got saved, but as she knelt there, she got a second blessing. She heard the voice of God. God said to her, "Do you remember the woman who let you borrow money fourteen years ago?"

She said, "Yes, Lord, I do remember."

God said, "I want you to pay it back. Restitution is what it is called, wherever possible."

She said, "Well, Lord, I will find out where she lives and I will send her a check."

God said, "No check. She needs the cash, and I not only want you to pay what you owe her but also give her six percent interest for fourteen years." God is a just God, isn't He?

She said, "But, Lord, I don't know how to get in touch with her."

God told her the phone number! God even knows your telephone number. He knows your deadline — and where to find you in time to meet it. He said, "She needs it by ten o'clock in the morning."

The lady who was about to be evicted went to her old friend's house, got her money, and got back a few minutes before ten o'clock. The constable was there. She put four months back rent on the table and four months in advance. The constable tore up the notice to evict.

When the lady finished her story, I just had one question for her, "Aren't you glad you trusted God?"

Hallelujah! You don't have any trouble. All you need is faith in God!

21
Oxygen Tank Miracle

A young seventeen-year-old girl in New York was dying with tuberculosis. One lung had collapsed. The other one was half gone. She was in an oxygen tank.

She attended a denominational church. The folks in her church loved God and were saved. However, they didn't believe in divine healing. Of course, divine healing doesn't make us Christians. The Blood of Jesus makes us Christians because He paid the price for our salvation at Calvary.

This young girl was dying. Her physician, who was a Christian, told her, "You are going to die and there is nothing we can do. Tuberculosis has set in. One lung is gone. The other is half gone. I am going to send you home so that you can spend your remaining days with your family."

She was breathing pure oxygen. She lay in an oxygen tent waiting for death — seventeen years old and had dwindled to sixty-seven pounds. She was a lovely young lady, but she was wasting away. Don't you tell me God does that to folks. I wouldn't serve a God who did that. God is a good God. He promises beauty for ashes.

> **The thief cometh not, but for to steal, and to kill, and to destroy: I am come that they might have life, and that they might have it more abundantly.**
>
> **John 10:10**

The doctor sent the girl home to die. She lay there with her head up, so she could read her Bible. She resigned herself to the fact that she was going to die. This is what she had been taught. You are only what you are taught. That is why you have to be careful where you go to church. I can't say that strongly enough. The girl lay in that position, reading Peter's epistle, **Who his own self bare our sins in his own body on the tree, that we, being dead to sins, should live unto righteousness...** (1 Peter 2:24). When she read those words, she put her Bible down and began to praise God.

Weeping, she said, "Oh, Lord, I will be so glad to see You. I know I am going to die. Doctors can't do any more for me. But thank You for saving me. Thank You for washing me in the blood." She worshiped and thanked God for saving her and went back to reading the same verse she had just read in her Bible.

His own self bare our sins in his own body on the tree, that we, being dead to sins, should live unto righteousness. . . . But she didn't stop there this time. She went right on in that same verse, **. . .by whose stripes ye were healed.** The words lit up like a neon sign. She said, "Oh, look what I found." There was no preacher there to preach to her. No one was there but the Word. She said, "Lord, I just finished praising You for that first part, now I am going to praise You for the second part. You have already healed me. Jesus, I am sorry I won't be seeing You right now. I plan on staying around here awhile."

Isn't that beautiful faith? Hallelujah! "I won't be coming like I planned," she said. "I have changed my mind, because I just found some truth — and truth is what sets us free." She started praising God for perfect health. She didn't gain weight instantly. She still weighed sixty-seven pounds. She unzipped that oxygen tent and hollered for her mother. "Mama, come quick!"

Her mother thought this was the day her daughter was going to die. She came stumbling up the stairs. "What is it, baby? What is it?"

"Oh, Mama, look what I found. Read this."

Her mother mumbled through the words, then said, "I read it. Lay down now."

The daughter said, "Oh, you didn't read it right. Won't you read it? Mama, it says I am healed. Two thousand years ago Jesus healed me."

Isn't it strange how some people can read it and get nothing out of it? The mother looked at her daughter and started crying.

"What is wrong, Mama, what are you crying about?"

"The doctor told me that on the day you were to die, you would lose your mind."

Isn't it strange that when you want to trust God, people think you are losing your mind? When you are willing to die, you are normal. "It is all right to get religious, but you don't have to carry that too far. Don't be a fanatic!" You don't have to believe that.

Her mother tucked her back in. But the girl said, "Mama, I am not going to die. Go downstairs and make me breakfast. I want some bacon and eggs, orange juice, whole wheat toast and coffee."

Mama said, "Now, I know you have lost your mind. You haven't eaten anything in ten months."

She said, "I haven't heard such powerful truth in ten months. Go down and make my breakfast, I am getting out of here."

The girl's mother tucked her in and sneaked out of the room. No sooner had she closed that door than the girl unzipped the oxygen tent. She pulled her scrawny legs out of the bed and hobbled over to her dresser. She took one of the dresses that she had worn when she was a hundred and twenty pounds. It looked like a robe on her now. She put slippers on her feet and started down the stairs. She went to the kitchen, opened that door and asked, "Are my bacon and eggs ready?" She sat down to have breakfast and said, "Lord, bless this food to my brand-new body. I am not going to die, I am going to live."

She went to her doctor the next day. The X-rays found two brand-new lungs and no sign of tuberculosis. She is now living in New York. She is married and has given birth to four children. She is going strong because she heard the truth.

People say, "My church doesn't believe it" — but neither did hers. Her mother wouldn't even believe with her. You don't need anybody — all you need is the Word of God. Stand on that Word.

22

Man Wrapped in Sheet

I was preaching in Houston, Texas, when a woman walked into my meeting with a sheet on her shoulder. I wondered what she had in that sheet. It wasn't long before I found out because she walked down the center aisle and dropped it at my feet. I was preaching — she was messing up my service! When she opened the sheet, there was a man in it — her husband. He weighed only fifty-eight pounds.

She said, "My husband used to weigh 200 pounds." Now he looked like a human skeleton. The stench of the man's disease almost knocked me out. I knew it was cancer. The woman looked at me and said, "It took me all night to get here, preacher. Now do what God called you to do. Heal this man."

These are the types of situations that help you find out whether you are called and sent, or whether you just went.

Do you believe God is going to disappoint that kind of faith? I wasn't about to lay hands. The Bible says we are to lay hands suddenly on no man. I was going to find out about this guy.

The woman said, "I come from New Orleans. The doctor told me yesterday my husband has seventy-two hours to live. One of those days is already shot. That means we only have forty-eight hours. When the doctor told me the news, I told him I was taking my husband to Houston. He told me there was no use in taking him to Houston. He thought I wanted to bring him here to the cancer specialists, and he said they would give me the same bottom line — that my husband is going to die. I just told the doctor, 'That is what you think.'"

That is the truth about faith, isn't it? Sometimes you have to stand alone.

The doctor told her he wouldn't let her move the patient, but she said, "He is my husband. I will sign him out." That is the kind of woman to have. Most women would try to get rid of the old rascal. But she said, "He is my man. I am not going to let that devil have him."

The doctor said, "Those specialists are going to give you the same diagnosis I did."

She said, "I am not taking him to a specialist. I am taking him to a man of God."

He said, "A what?"

"A man of God."

He said, "I don't believe in that."

She said, "You don't have to. He is my man. I believe in it. That is the bottom line."

Let every man, let every devil be a liar, but let God be true! If He said it, He will do it, and if He spoke it, He will bring it to pass!

She said, "I am going to sign him out."

The doctor said, "I will hide his clothes."

She said, "I will steal a sheet."

I looked at the sheet, and it had the name of the hospital on it. She had stolen it! Faith never gives up. Faith will find a way. Faith presses on. Faith takes the answer from God. Faith never sits in a pew. Faith steps out on the water. Faith steps out on the Word. Faith says, "Yes, Lord, I am going to take the answer." God can't lie. I believe what He said.

She said, "Brother Schambach, let's dispense with the talking now. Lay your hands on him."

I couldn't stand to look at him because the stench was coming right at my face. I had to turn my face, but I touched him. I said, "You foul devil. I curse you at the roots in the name of Jesus, and I command you to die and pass from this man's body."

That man was only in his late forties. The devil kills people before their time. The thief comes to steal, to kill, to destroy. I could see the marks of the devil on that body but I refused to let the devil have him. I said, "In the name of Jesus, I reverse it." I threw the sheet on him and said, "Get him out of here. He is well."

He didn't get up and walk. He only weighed fifty-eight pounds — skin and bones. The woman picked him up, threw him right back over her shoulder, walked out, didn't even stay for the offering. Halfway back, she turned around and said, "Bye, Brother Schambach. See you when you get to New Orleans."

Six months later we put the tent up in New Orleans. During the opening night, I saw a big man enter. He was six foot one and weighed 200 pounds. He wore a brand-new blue suit. I didn't know who he was. He walked up on the ramp, and I wondered why my men let him get up there. The Holy Ghost must have frozen them right in their spot. We don't let anybody up on the platform. All of a sudden, this guy grabbed me and lifted me off the ground. I said, "Put me down."

He said, "I am the man who was in the sheet."

I said, "Pick me back up again. Let's dance!"

Isn't that beautiful? Six months later, he was back to his normal weight. He hadn't even known his wife had taken him to Houston. He was just about gone, forty-eight hours to live. When she took him back to the doctor, they examined him and couldn't find a trace of cancer anywhere. When I spoke to that cancer, I spoke resurrection life into his body. I spoke to that mountain. I spoke in faith believing God was going to do it. I called it done. If God says He is the healer, I have a right to pronounce him healed. Speak it into existence in the name of Jesus!

> **For we wrestle not against flesh and blood, but against principalities, against powers, against the rulers of the darkness of this world, against spiritual wickedness in high places.**
>
> **Ephesians 6:12**

> **And five of you shall chase an hundred, and an hundred of you shall put ten thousand to flight: and your enemies shall fall before you by the sword.**
>
> **Leviticus 26:8**

Why?

> **Ye are of God, little children, and have overcome them: because greater is he that is in you, than he that is in the world.**
>
> **1 John 4:4**

23

R.W. Battles the Devil

I was on the turnpike, driving from Philadelphia to Chicago. I had plenty of time in the car. I was speaking in tongues, prophesying and dancing. Have you ever danced while you were driving? It was just me and Jesus in that car. Just me and Jesus, having time together. No one was around to say, "You aren't in the Spirit." Just me and Jesus in that automobile.

I was halfway through Ohio, when all of a sudden a pain struck me in the fifth rib. I doubled over the steering wheel. At that moment, my foot hit the brake.

Ol' Slewfoot was sitting on my shoulder. "Heart trouble," he whispered.

I wondered how he got in the car with all the tongue speaking, prophesying and shouting. How did that devil get in here?

I pulled over to the shoulder of the road, and engaged the devil in a conversation. He asked, "How many people did you bury this week?"

I was still doubled over, but I thought of all the funerals I had preached at that week. "Four of them," I said.

"What did they die from?" he asked.

Every time that devil jumps on you, he knows how to mess your faith up — even while you are speaking in tongues. He said, "How many of your brothers have died?"

I said, "There's Ruben, Henry, Charles — four?"

"What did they die from?"

If I had seen a grave, I would have jumped in it. That's how bad it hurt! Then I came to my senses and said, "You filthy, rotten, lying devil. You are a liar. How can I have heart trouble when Jesus lives in there?"

He said, "Still hurts, doesn't it?"

I said, "Let it hurt. I am healed anyway. If God said I am healed, then I am, healing is mine."

I pulled the keys out of the ignition. I locked the car and said, "Slewfoot, wait here. I will be back. If I have heart trouble, I won't see you again. I am going to run down this turnpike, I am going to jog until I get my second wind." I took off running — until I got my second wind. I felt so good as I was coming back that if I would have seen Mohammed Ali, I believe I could have whipped him right then.

When I got back to the car, I couldn't find the devil anywhere. I said, "Where are you, devil? Where are you? I want you to know, I am healed!"

But the devil was long gone. Only Jesus was there.

But he [Jesus] was wounded for our transgressions, he was bruised for our iniquities: the chastisement of our peace was upon him; and with his stripes we are healed.

Isaiah 53:5

24

Spit in My Eyes

A black lady, who had been blind for thirty-eight years, was in New York City. She was standing in line ready to receive prayer. There were about 500 people to pray for — and the ushers brought her first. After I prayed, I said, "I believe God it is done. You are healed."

She said, "No, I am not."

I put my arm to her back and I tried to move her along, but she just dug in. She said, "I am not going anywhere. You didn't do what God told me to tell you to do."

I said, "Take it by faith."

She said, "No." Women can be stubborn. She just stayed there. She said, "Brother Schambach, God told me to tell you to do something. I am not leaving here until you do it."

I said, "All right, what did He tell you?"

She said, "He told me to tell you to spit in my eyes."

I said, "I am not going to do that. It isn't sanitary. It isn't healthy. I am not going to do it."

She said, "Yes, you are, because I am not leaving until you do. God told me to tell you to do this."

She wouldn't budge. I said, "I won't do it. I am not spitting on you."

She said, "Brother Schambach, I am tired of being blind. Jesus did this to heal a blind man. Are you better than Jesus?"

She knew how to hurt a guy. I said, "I am going to find out if God really spoke to you."

She wouldn't give up. Thank God for women who don't give up. Don't you take no for an answer. If you find something in the Book, stick by your guns. Say, "Devil, you are a liar." Show your faith to God. Say, "God, look what You said here. You can't lie. If You said it, then it belongs to me. I am going to write my name right there on the side of the margin, 'Lord, it belongs to me.' "

The woman refused to give up. She knew God's voice. I began to weep. But I did what God had told her should be done. And the moment I did, the power of God hit her. For the first time in 38 years, twenty-twenty vision came back to her eyes. She ran around that building!

Don't give up. Don't give up. Whatever He says for you to do, do it. God is looking for obedience.

25
Highway Bridge Miracle

I don't like hotels. If I am preaching close to home, I like to return to my own bed. We were living in the Valley Forge, Pennsylvania, area. After a meeting in New York, at about midnight, I was driving home. It was a two-and-a-half hour drive. It was raining. I had the car on cruise control. My CB radio was on; my handle is "Good News." Everyone on the CB wants to know what the good news is, so I start preaching and they find out!

That night I was passing a tractor trailer and the driver said, "Is that you coming up on me, preacher?"

I said, "That's me."

He said, "Everything is clear. Go through."

I passed his rig. The rain was coming down. The windshield wipers were on. I was still on cruise control, about fifty-five miles an hour. I know that is too fast on wet ground, but it was so early in the morning, and there was very little traffic.

Suddenly, in front of me, I saw a woman with a white sweater in a green automobile. I don't know what had happened to her, but the car was sitting sideways, blocking both lanes. I was on a bridge, so there was no shoulder.

There I was, with one eye on the rear-view mirror looking at that eighteen-wheeler coming up on me, and a car in my path on the bridge. There was no way out. It was an impossible situation. Have you ever found yourself in an impossible situation? You don't have time to bow down.

There's only one thing you have time to do, that is to holler, "Jesus!"

When I hollered, my right foot came on the brake. All four wheels grabbed and went into a slide. I knew there was no way out. I already had the distance measured. I hit the brakes a second time and shouted a second time, "Jesus!" This time, the tires grabbed. But that eighteen-wheeler was still coming up behind me, and I felt like a piece of cheese in a sandwich.

I knew if the trucker hit his brakes, the rig was going to jackknife and make mincemeat out of me, so I hollered one more time. What did I holler? "Jesus!" Don't you love that name? There's power in that name. I looked in my rear-view mirror, and the truck had not even put on his brakes. He was still coming. All of a sudden, he came up alongside of me, went by me, by the car, by the bridge, and never hit a thing. How did that happen?

Within moments, a half dozen more eighteen-wheelers came rolling up. They saw the situation, moved up slowly and stopped. They measured. They couldn't get through. Only one got through — and just barely. They were all the same size, but only one had the nerve to squeak through.

Down the road, the first trucker stopped and came walking back. "Are you the preacher?" he asked.

I said, "Yes, sir."

He took his hat off in the rain, scratching his head. He said, "How did I do it?"

I said, "You wouldn't believe it if I told you."

He said, "Try me, preacher."

I said, "When I saw you coming, I knew you couldn't see."

He said, "I didn't see that car. I saw your brake lights when they went on. After that I saw the car. But if I had put my brakes on, I would have had you."

I said, "Brother, I hollered Jesus three times. That's all I had time to do. Jesus has a great big bridge stretcher up there!"

Jesus is in the impossible place. He will make a way where there is no way. If you are hooked on drugs, He will set you free. If you are bound by alcohol, He will set you free. If you need the baptism of the Holy Ghost, He will fill you with power!

He is the way!

26
The Girl Who Read Her Bible

I pioneered a church in Chicago. I was pastoring there when the Supreme Court took the Bible out of schools. Christians basically sat there in their upholstered pews and did nothing about it. This is the reason why our nation is in the mess that it is today. When they took the Bible out of schools, humanistic philosophy took its place.

There was a sixteen-year-old girl who came to my church at that time. She didn't consult with me. She didn't consult with her parents. Do you know what she did the day after the Supreme Court made this announcement official? She said, "The devil is a liar." She got up for school the next morning and took her Bible.

She attended one of the largest high schools in Chicago. During the school assembly, in front of 3,700 students, she walked to the platform, climbed the steps and walked to the rostrum.

"The Supreme Court says it is illegal for me to read the Bible in a public school," she announced. "Now I will read from St. Mark's gospel, chapter five." That is my kind of girl. All the teachers sat there with their mouths hanging open. Nobody stopped her and she read the entire chapter.

All those kids thought, "I wish I could get some of what she is smoking," because they were looking for the ultimate high. At first, they thought she was on drugs. She wasn't defying the school authorities, she was defying the Supreme Court of the United States.

They arrested her. She was let out on bail, but the next day she went to school again with her Bible. There is no place in God's army for a bunch of sissies. If you want to be a sissy, go serve the devil. God is looking for men and women who are not afraid to get in the fight, eyeball the devil and let him know that *greater is he that is in* [me], *than he that is in the world.* (1 John 4:4b.)

This time the reporters were there. They thought she would do it again. Her teachers wouldn't even stop her. The principal was sitting there. The girl walked up to the rostrum and opened her Bible and said, "This morning I am reading from Matthew's account."

Hallelujah! Hallelujah! God used these episodes to turn young people on to Him. The authorities arrested her again. She did it again and again and again. They couldn't stop her. She could have taken her place with the rest of the church. She could have been passive about it and said, "Well, it is the law." But she didn't.

Finally, the school authorities said, "How would you like to have your own classroom after school? Then, you can read the Bible as much as you want."

They announced it to the student body, and the first day she had a class of 750. Attending her class were drug addicts who wanted to know what somebody was shooting into her. That girl was on a high, and they respected her because she was not afraid of the consequences. They wanted to find out what she was on. She let them know right away that she was on a permanent high. She was washed in the blood of the Lamb and filled with the Holy Ghost and with fire.

Revival broke out in that school. You see, the devil has no sense. He had the Bible taken out of the school, and God put living epistles in the school to follow the teachings of the written ones. Kids started to get saved. The teachers came down to find out what was going on. . .and they got saved too! They were filled with the Holy Ghost. Some of them are in the ministry today. All because of one sixteen-year-old girl, who had the courage to take a stand for God.

27

Car Accident in Baltimore

Some time ago, I was holding a crusade in Baltimore, Maryland. My first meeting was on Harford Road. Before the first afternoon service, I took my briefcase out of the car and walked to the auditorium. Suddenly, I heard screeching tires coming around a corner, then a crash. I thought a car had hit an animal, maybe a dog.

No, it was a little child.

The car dragged the little boy about two blocks down Harford Road.

Instead of going into the building where the people were assembled, I found myself running after that automobile. By the time I caught up to it, a crowd had assembled. A police officer was there, and the boy was lying in a pool of blood. The body was convulsing.

I am not ashamed of the name of Jesus. I made up my mind about that a long time ago. Only those people who cuss and use His name in vain should be ashamed. I am not ashamed to heal the sick using that name, right on the sidewalk.

So, with boldness, I went through the crowd. They were standing there watching the boy convulsing, and the police officer took his jacket off to make a pillow for the boy. I knelt beside him.

I said to the officer, "Do you mind if I pray for the young fellow?"

He said, "Are you a minister?"

I said, "Yes."

He said, "Go ahead, preacher. It looks bad."

I cradled that boy in my arms and began to pray. I could feel those hot darts coming from the eyes of those people. I shouted it out loud, "In the name of Jesus!" I thought, "Bless God, if they don't go to church, they are going to be in church right now."

I was going to take advantage of this situation. I prayed, "Jesus, You called me to use Your name. You said that if I lay hands on the sick in Your name, they shall recover. In the name of Jesus, I command the blood to coagulate. I command the bleeding to stop and the convulsions to cease. Lord, if there are any broken bones, heal them. Put every muscle, every piece of tissue, every vein back together again. Totally restore this boy to health, and don't allow any damage to remain in his body."

When I finished praying, the convulsions had stopped. The boy opened his eyes, looked up at me, and said, "Thank you, preacher."

The ambulance came, picked him up and took him to the hospital. I returned to my meeting wearing a bloody suit and began to preach.

As the evening service was about to begin, I spotted that little boy on the front row with his father, mother and seven or eight brothers and sisters. The little boy stood up and said, "Daddy, that's the man. That's the man of God. Right there. He is the one who prayed for me on the street corner."

The man came over to me with tears running down his face. He said, "I want to shake the hand of a man who is not ashamed to pray for someone on the street corner." He looked me in the eye and said, "I want to know this Jesus that you have in you."

I led that whole family to Jesus Christ. They were the first converts of that Baltimore meeting. Today they are still members of my friend's church. There is power in the name of Jesus!

28
Healing of Crossed Eyes

We were setting up a tent in Sacramento, California, and getting ready for an afternoon service. A woman brought her child, who had crossed eyes, for prayer. I saw her weeping in the back so I went to her and said, "What is wrong?"

"Oh," she said, "I brought my daughter who has had crossed eyes since birth. I came from San Francisco for a prayer card but you aren't having a service. I have traveled hundreds of miles. What am I going to do? I knew if I could just get her under the tent, her eyes would be healed."

I said, "Where is your daughter?"

The mother, sobbing, gestured to a little girl nearby. "Here she is." I got down on my knees and looked at the little girl's face — and saw two straight eyes.

I said, "Are you sure this is your daughter?"

"I ought to know my own daughter," she replied.

I said, "You told me she had crossed eyes."

The mother got down on her knees and looked at her daughter's eyes. No one laid hands on the girl. She didn't have to get a prayer card. She grabbed that girl and started running around the tent. God had performed a miracle. When did God do it? God took her at her word. I heard her say, "I knew if I could just get my daughter under that tent. . . ." I believe the moment she stepped inside that tent, the crossed eyes became straight because God honored her faith.

29

The Greatest Miracle of All

Everywhere I go, I tell people, "God has a miracle with your name on it." Sometimes I encourage people to tell those sitting next to them in the service, "Tonight is my night for a miracle."

Why do I do that? I want people to know that the same Jesus that God raised from the dead — the same Jesus who opened blind eyes and made the crippled walk — is alive today. God is a miracle-working God!

Jesus Christ the same yesterday, and to day, and for ever.

Hebrews 13:8

Sometimes we have more faith in the miracles of science and technology than we do in the power of the living Christ. But no one can make me doubt His power.

So many times I have told people that the greatest miracle of all is when God replaces a heart of stone with a heart of flesh.

As a young lad, I ran from God. I was busy going nowhere. One day, while rushing to get on with business, I was stopped in my tracks by the greatest news I ever heard in my life.

All of a sudden, over a loud speaker, a street preacher, Brother Anthony Vigna, cried out, "Hey sinner!"

I stopped. I thought, "Who knows me around here?"

Then came those life-changing words, "You don't have to sin anymore!" I was a seventeen-year-old boy running from God, but I heard the words that brought freedom from guilt and from the bondage of sin.

I knelt down on the sidewalk a sinner. I asked Christ to forgive me, to cleanse me, to come into my life and to walk and talk in me. I told Jesus I had turned my back on sin.

When I stood up, I had been cleansed and forgiven. I was now a child of God. What a miracle! In an instant, I had passed from death to life.

God wants to open your blind eyes, deliver you from drugs, heal your suffering body, put your marriage back together and free you from guilt and depression. But He can't release His full miracle-working power through your life until He has your heart.

You can give Him your heart right now, by praying this simple prayer:

Lord Jesus, I confess I am a sinner and in need of a Savior. I receive what took place at Calvary as my very own. Come into my life and make me Yours. I pray to be born again and made new by Your Spirit. I thank You for it now. Amen.

Go and tell someone what you have done. You have received the gift of salvation. You have been born again. You have received the greatest miracle of all!

30

The Miracles of Christ

Jesus began His public ministry as a ministry of miracles. Everything about His life involved miracles: His conception, birth, life, wisdom and teachings, ministry, death, resurrection, appearances, and ascension — all of these were astounding and undeniable miracles.

Many people have said that miracles were just for the days of the Old and New Testaments, but that is not true. Jesus Christ is as much a miracle-worker now as He ever was; and people need His miracle touch now more than ever.

We are called to walk as the Christians did in the New Testament. To serve the needs of people today. Jesus must be allowed to live in us, in His power and with His personal presence guiding us.

When people act on God's Word in bold faith, the faith which produces miracles, then multitudes come from miles around, eager to see Christ's miracle power in demonstration.

Jesus always attracted the multitudes by His miracles then and He does so today, wherever miracles are done in His name. He is the same yesterday, today and forever.

If we preach as the early Church preached, we will get the same results that they got: miracles and healings. It doesn't matter where we are or who we are. If we want to get Bible results, we have to preach what the Bible says: that miracles are a part of the present-day ministry of Jesus Christ.

The Miracles

1. Turning the Water to Wine

And the third day there was a marriage in Cana of Galilee; and the mother of Jesus was there: And both Jesus was called, and his disciples, to the marriage. And when they wanted wine, the mother of Jesus saith unto him, They have no wine.

Jesus saith unto her, Woman, what have I to do with thee? mine hour is not yet come. His mother saith unto the servants, Whatsoever he saith unto you, do it. And there were set there six waterpots of stone, after the manner of the purifying of the Jews, containing two or three firkins apiece.

Jesus saith unto them, Fill the waterpots with water. And they filled them up to the brim. And he saith unto them, Draw out now, and bear unto the governor of the feast. And they bare it. When the ruler of the feast had tasted the water that was made wine, and knew not whence it was: (but the servants which drew the water knew;) the governor of the feast called the bridegroom,

And saith unto him, Every man at the beginning doth set forth good wine; and when men have well drunk, then that which is worse: but thou hast kept the good wine until now. This beginning of miracles did Jesus in Cana of Galilee, and manifested forth his glory; and his disciples believed on him.

John 2:1-11

2. Nobleman's Son Healed

So Jesus came again into Cana of Galilee, where he made the water wine. And there was a certain nobleman, whose son was sick at Capernaum. When he heard that Jesus was come out of Judaea into Galilee, he went unto him, and besought him that he would come down, and heal his son: for he was at the point of death.

Then said Jesus unto him, Except ye see signs and wonders, ye will not believe. The nobleman saith unto him, Sir, come down ere my child die. Jesus saith unto him, Go thy way; thy son liveth. And the man believed the word that Jesus had spoken unto him, and he went his way.

And as he was now going down, his servants met him, and told him, saying, Thy son liveth. Then enquired he of them the hour when he began to amend. And they said unto him, Yesterday at the seventh hour the fever left him. So the father knew that it was at the same hour, in the which Jesus said unto him, Thy son liveth: and himself believed, and his whole house.

This is again the second miracle that Jesus did, when he was come out of Judaea into Galilee.

John 4:46-54

3. The Draught of Fishes

Now when he had left speaking, he said unto Simon, Launch out into the deep, and let down your nets for a draught. And Simon answering said unto him, Master, we have toiled all the night, and have taken nothing: nevertheless at thy word I will let down the net. And when they had this done, they inclosed a great multitude of fishes: and their net brake.

And they beckoned unto their partners, which were in the other ship, that they should come and help them. And they came, and filled both the ships, so that they began to sink. When Simon Peter saw it, he fell down at Jesus' knees, saying, Depart from me; for I am a sinful man, O Lord. For he was astonished, and all that were with him, at the draught of the fishes which they had taken.

Luke 5:4-9

4. Healing the Demoniac

And there was in their synagogue a man with an unclean spirit; and he cried out, Saying, Let us alone; what have we to do with thee, thou Jesus of Nazareth? art thou come to destroy us? I know thee who thou art, the Holy One of God.

And Jesus rebuked him, saying, Hold thy peace, and come out of him. And when the unclean spirit had torn him, and cried with a loud voice, he came out of him. And they were all amazed, insomuch that they questioned among themselves, saying, What thing is this? what new doctrine is this? for with authority commandeth he even the unclean spirits, and they do obey him.

And immediately his fame spread abroad throughout all the region round about Galilee.

Mark 1:23-28

5. Healing Peter's Mother-in-Law

And forthwith, when they were come out of the synagogue, they entered into the house of Simon and Andrew, with James and John. But Simon's wife's mother lay sick of a fever, and anon they tell him of her. And he came and took her by the hand, and lifted her up; and immediately the fever left her, and she ministered unto them.

Mark 1:29-31

6. Healing of the Leper

And, behold, there came a leper and worshipped him, saying, Lord, if thou wilt, thou canst make me clean. And Jesus put forth his hand, and touched him, saying, I will; be thou clean. And immediately his leprosy was cleansed. And Jesus saith unto him, See thou tell no man; but go thy way, shew thyself to the priest, and offer the gift that Moses commanded, for a testimony unto them.

Matthew 8:2-4

7. Healing the Paralytic

And straightway many were gathered together, insomuch that there was no room to receive them, no, not so much as about the door: and he preached the word unto them. And they come unto him, bringing one sick of the palsy, which was borne of four. And when they could not come nigh unto him for the press, they uncovered the roof where he was: and when they had broken it up, they let down the bed wherein the sick of the palsy lay.

When Jesus saw their faith, he said unto the sick of the palsy, Son, thy sins be forgiven thee. But there was certain of the scribes sitting there, and reasoning in their hearts, Why doth this man thus speak blasphemies? who can forgive sins but God only?

And immediately when Jesus perceived in his spirit that they so reasoned within themselves, he said unto them, Why reason ye these things in your hearts? Whether is it easier to say to the sick of the palsy, Thy sins be forgiven thee; or to say, Arise, and take up thy bed, and walk? But that ye may know that the Son of man hath power on earth to forgive sins, (he saith to the sick of the palsy,) I say unto thee, Arise, and take up thy bed, and go thy way into thine house.

And immediately he arose, took up the bed, and went forth before them all; insomuch that they were all amazed, and glorified God, saying, We never saw it on this fashion.

Mark 2:2-12

8. Healing the Man at the Pool

Now there is at Jerusalem by the sheep market a pool, which is called in the Hebrew tongue Bethesda, having five porches. In these lay a great multitude of impotent folk, of blind, halt, withered, waiting for the moving of the water. For an angel went down at a certain season into the pool, and troubled the water: whosoever then first after the troubling of the water stepped in was made whole of whatsoever disease he had.

And a certain man was there, which had an infirmity thirty and eight years. When Jesus saw him lie, and knew that he had been now a long time in that case, he saith unto him, Wilt thou be made whole? The impotent man answered him, Sir, I have no man, when the water is troubled, to put me into the pool: but while I am coming, another steppeth down before me. Jesus saith unto him, Rise, take up thy bed, and walk. And immediately the man was made whole, and took up his bed, and walked: and on the same day was the sabbath.

John 5:2-9

9. Healing the Withered Hand

And when he was departed thence, he went into their synagogue: And, behold, there was a man which had his hand withered. And they asked him, saying, Is it lawful to heal on the sabbath days? that they might accuse him.

And he said unto them, What man shall there be among you, that shall have one sheep, and if it fall into a pit on the sabbath day, will he not lay hold on it, and lift it out? How much then is a man better than a sheep? Wherefore it is lawful to do well on the sabbath days. Then saith he to the man, Stretch forth thine hand. And he stretched it forth; and it was restored whole, like as the other.

Matthew 12:9-13

10. Healing Many Near Galilee

But Jesus withdrew himself with his disciples to the sea: and a great multitude from Galilee followed him, and from

Judaea, And from Jerusalem, and from Idumaea, and from beyond Jordan; and they about Tyre and Sidon, a great multitude, when they had heard what great things he did, came unto him.

And he spake to his disciples, that a small ship should wait on him because of the multitude, lest they should throng him. For he had healed many; insomuch that they pressed upon him for to touch him, as many as had plagues. And unclean spirits, when they saw him, fell down before him, and cried, saying, Thou art the Son of God. And he straitly charged them that they should not make him known.

Mark 3:7-12

11. Healing the Centurion's Servant

And a certain centurion's servant, who was dear unto him, was sick, and ready to die. And when he heard of Jesus, he sent unto him the elders of the Jews, beseeching him that he would come and heal his servant. And when they came to Jesus, they besought him instantly, saying, That he was worthy for whom he should do this: For he loveth our nation, and he hath built us a synagogue.

Then Jesus went with them. And when he was now not far from the house, the centurion sent friends to him, saying unto him, Lord, trouble not thyself: for I am not worthy that thou shouldest enter under my roof: Wherefore neither thought I myself worthy to come unto thee: but say in a word, and my servant shall be healed. For I also am a man set under authority, having under me soldiers, and I say unto one, Go, and he goeth; and to another, Come, and he cometh; and to my servant, Do this, and he doeth it.

When Jesus heard these things, he marvelled at him, and turned him about, and said unto the people that followed him, I say unto you, I have not found so great faith, no, not in Israel. And they that were sent, returning to the house, found the servant whole that had been sick.

Luke 7:2-10

12. Raising the Widow's Son

Now when he came nigh to the gate of the city, behold, there was a dead man carried out, the only son of his mother, and she was a widow: and much people of the city was with her. And when the Lord saw her, he had compassion on her, and said unto her, Weep not. And he came and touched the bier: and they that bare him stood still. And he said, Young man, I say unto thee, Arise. And he that was dead sat up, and began to speak. And he delivered him to his mother.

And there came a fear on all: and they glorified God, saying, That a great prophet is risen up among us; and, That God hath visited his people.

Luke 7:12-16

13. Healing the Dumb Demoniac Man

Then was brought unto him one possessed with a devil, blind, and dumb: and he healed him, insomuch that the blind and dumb both spake and saw.

Matthew 12:22

14. Calming the Tempest

And, behold, there arose a great tempest in the sea, insomuch that the ship was covered with the waves: but he was asleep. And his disciples came to him, and awoke him, saying, Lord, save us: we perish.

And he saith unto them, Why are ye fearful, O ye of little faith? Then he arose, and rebuked the winds and the sea; and there was a great calm. But the men marvelled, saying, What manner of man is this, that even the winds and the sea obey him!

Matthew 8:24-27

15. Healing the Gadarene Demoniac

And they came over unto the other side of the sea, into the country of the Gadarenes. And when he was come out of the ship, immediately there met him out of the tombs a man with an unclean spirit, Who had his dwelling among the tombs; and no man could bind him, no, not with chains: Because that he had been often bound with fetters and chains, and the chains had been plucked asunder by him, and the fetters broken in pieces: neither could any man tame him.

And always, night and day, he was in the mountains, and in the tombs, crying, and cutting himself with stones. But when he saw Jesus afar off, he ran and worshipped him, And cried with a loud voice, and said, What have I to do with thee, Jesus, thou Son of the most high God? I adjure thee by God, that thou torment me not. For he said unto him, Come out of the man, thou unclean spirit.

And he asked him, What is thy name? And he answered, saying, My name is Legion: for we are many. And he besought him much that he would not send them away out of the country. Now there was there nigh unto the mountains a great herd of swine feeding. And all the devils besought him, saying, Send us into the swine, that we may enter into them.

And forthwith Jesus gave them leave. And the unclean spirits went out, and entered into the swine: and the herd ran violently down a steep place into the sea, (they were about two thousand;) and were choked in the sea. And they that fed the swine fled, and told it in the city, and in the country. And they went out to see what it was that was done. And they come to Jesus, and see him that was possessed with the devil, and had the legion, sitting, and clothed, and in his right mind: and they were afraid. And they that saw it told them how it befell to him that was possessed with the devil, and also concerning the swine.

And they began to pray him to depart out of their coasts. And when he was come into the ship, he that had been possessed with the devil prayed him that he might be with him. Howbeit Jesus suffered him not, but saith unto him, Go home to thy friends, and tell them how great things the Lord hath done for thee, and hath had compassion on thee. And he departed, and began to publish in Decapolis how great things Jesus had done for him: and all men did marvel.

Mark 5:1-20

16. Healing the Afflicted Woman

And a woman having an issue of blood twelve years, which had spent all her living upon physicians, neither could be healed of any, Came behind him, and touched the border of his garment: and immediately her issue of blood stanched. And Jesus said, Who touched me? When all denied, Peter and they that were with him said, Master, the multitude throng thee and press thee, and sayest thou, Who touched me? And Jesus said, Somebody hath touched me: for I perceive that virtue is gone out of me.

And when the woman saw that she was not hid, she came trembling, and falling down before him, she declared unto him before all the people for what cause she had touched him, and how she was healed immediately. And he said unto her, Daughter, be of good comfort: thy faith hath made thee whole; go in peace.

Luke 8:43-48

17. Raising Jairus' Daughter

While he spake these things unto them, behold, there came a certain ruler, and worshipped him, saying, My daughter is even now dead: but come and lay thy hand upon her, and she shall live. And Jesus arose, and followed him, and so did his disciples.

And when Jesus came into the ruler's house, and saw the minstrels and the people making a noise, He said unto them, Give place: for the maid is not dead, but sleepeth. And they laughed him to scorn. But when the people were put forth, he went in, and took her by the hand, and the maid arose.

And the fame hereof went abroad into all that land.

Matthew 9:18,19,23-26

18. Healing the Blind Man and the Dumb Man

And when Jesus departed thence, two blind men followed him, crying, and saying, Thou son of David, have mercy on us. And when he was come into the house, the blind men came to him: and Jesus saith unto them, Believe ye that I am able to do this? They said unto him, Yea, Lord.

Then touched he their eyes, saying, According to your faith be it unto you. And their eyes were opened; and Jesus straitly charged them, saying, See that no man know it. But they, when they were departed, spread abroad his fame in all that country.

As they went out, behold, they brought to him a dumb man possessed with a devil. And when the devil was cast out, the dumb spake: and the multitudes marvelled, saying, It was never so seen in Israel. But the Pharisees said, He casteth out devils through the prince of the devils.

Matthew 9:27-34

19. Feeding the Five Thousand

When Jesus then lifted up his eyes, and saw a great company come unto him, he saith unto Philip, Whence shall we buy bread, that these may eat? And this he said to prove him: for he himself knew what he would do.

Philip answered him, Two hundred pennyworth of bread is not sufficient for them, that every one of them may take a little. One of his disciples, Andrew, Simon Peter's brother, saith unto him, There is a lad here, which hath five barley loaves, and two small fishes: but what are they among so many?

And Jesus said, Make the men sit down. Now there was much grass in the place. So the men sat down, in number about five thousand. And Jesus took the loaves; and when he had given thanks, he distributed to the disciples, and the disciples to them that were set down; and likewise of the fishes as much as they would.

When they were filled, he said unto his disciples, Gather up the fragments that remain, that nothing be lost. Therefore they gathered them together, and filled twelve baskets with the fragments of the five barley loaves, which remained over and above unto them that had eaten. Then those men, when they had seen the miracle that Jesus did, said, This is of a truth that prophet that should come into the world.

John 6:5-14

20. Walking on the Sea

And straightway he constrained his disciples to get into the ship, and to go to the other side before unto Bethsaida, while he sent away the people. And when he had sent them away, he departed into a mountain to pray. And when even was come, the ship was in the midst of the sea, and he alone on the land.

And he saw them toiling in rowing; for the wind was contrary unto them: and about the fourth watch of the night he cometh unto them, walking upon the sea, and would have passed by them. But when they saw him walking upon the sea, they supposed it had been a spirit, and cried out: For they all saw him, and were troubled. And immediately he talked with them, and saith unto them, Be of good cheer: it is I; be not afraid.

And he went up unto them into the ship; and the wind ceased: and they were sore amazed in themselves beyond measure, and wondered. For they considered not the miracle of the loaves: for their heart was hardened.

Mark 6:45-52

21. Performing Many Miracles

And when they were gone over, they came into the land of Gennesaret. And when the men of that place had knowledge of him, they sent out into all that country round about, and brought unto him all that were diseased; And besought him that they might only touch the hem of his garment: and as many as touched were made perfectly whole.

Matthew 14:34-36

22. Healing the Syrophoenician Woman's Daughter

And, behold, a woman of Canaan came out of the same coasts, and cried unto him, saying, Have mercy on me, O Lord, thou son of David; my daughter is grievously vexed with a devil. But he answered her not a word. And his disciples came and besought him, saying, Send her away; for she crieth after us. But he answered and said, I am not sent but unto the lost sheep of the house of Israel.

Then came she and worshipped him, saying, Lord, help me. But he answered and said, It is not meet to take the children's bread, and to cast it to dogs. And she said, Truth, Lord: yet the dogs eat of the crumbs which fall from their masters' table.

Then Jesus answered and said unto her, O woman, great is thy faith: be it unto thee even as thou wilt. And her daughter was made whole from that very hour.

Matthew 15:22-28

23. Healing the Deaf and Dumb Man

And they bring unto him one that was deaf, and had an impediment in his speech; and they beseech him to put his hand upon him. And he took him aside from the multitude, and put his fingers into his ears, and he spit, and touched his tongue; And looking up to heaven, he sighed, and saith unto him, Ephphatha, that is, Be opened. And straightway his ears were opened, and the string of his tongue was loosed, and he spake plain.

And he charged them that they should tell no man: but the more he charged them, so much the more a great deal they published it; And were beyond measure astonished, saying, He hath done all things well: he maketh both the deaf to hear, and the dumb to speak.

Mark 7:32-37

24. Performing Many Miracles

And Jesus departed from thence, and came nigh unto the sea of Galilee; and went up into a mountain, and sat down there. And great multitudes came unto him, having with them those that were lame, blind, dumb, maimed, and many others, and cast them down at Jesus' feet; and he healed them: Insomuch that the multitude wondered, when they saw the dumb to speak, the maimed to be whole, the lame to walk, and the blind to see: and they glorified the God of Israel.

Matthew 15:29-31

25. Feeding the Four Thousand

In those days the multitude being very great, and having nothing to eat, Jesus called his disciples unto him, and saith unto them, I have compassion on the multitude, because they have now been with me three days, and have nothing to eat: And if I send them away fasting to their own houses, they will faint by the way: for divers of them came from far.

And his disciples answered him, From whence can a man satisfy these men with bread here in the wilderness? And he asked them, How many loaves have ye? And they said, Seven. And he commanded the people to sit down on the ground: and he took the seven loaves, and gave thanks, and brake, and gave to his disciples to set before them; and they did set them before the people.

And they had a few small fishes: and he blessed, and commanded to set them also before them. So they did eat, and were filled: and they took up of the broken meat that was left seven baskets. And they that had eaten were about four thousand: and he sent them away.

Mark 8:1-9

26. Healing the Blind Man at Bethsaida

And he cometh to Bethsaida; and they bring a blind man unto him, and besought him to touch him. And he took the blind man by the hand, and led him out of the town; and when he had spit on his eyes, and put his hands upon him, he asked him if he saw ought.

And he looked up, and said, I see men as trees, walking. After that he put his hands again upon his eyes, and made him look up: and he was restored, and saw every man clearly. And he sent him away to his house, saying, Neither go into the town, nor tell it to any in the town.

Mark 8:22-26

27. Jesus' Transfiguration

And it came to pass about an eight days after these sayings, he took Peter and John and James, and went up into a mountain to pray. And as he prayed, the fashion of his countenance was altered, and his raiment was white and glistering. And, behold, there talked with him two men, which were Moses and Elias: Who appeared in glory, and spake of his decease which he should accomplish at Jerusalem.

But Peter and they that were with him were heavy with sleep: and when they were awake, they saw his glory, and the two men that stood with him. And it came to pass, as they departed from him, Peter said unto Jesus, Master, it is good for us to be here: and let us make three tabernacles; one for thee, and one for Moses, and one for Elias: not knowing what he said. While he thus spake, there came a cloud, and overshadowed them: and they feared as they entered into the cloud.

And there came a voice out of the cloud, saying, This is my beloved Son: hear him. And when the voice was past, Jesus was found alone. And they kept it close, and told no man in those days any of those things which they had seen.

Luke 9:28-36

28. Healing the Demoniac Son

And when they were come to the multitude, there came to him a certain man, kneeling down to him, and saying, Lord, have mercy on my son: for he is lunatick, and sore vexed: for ofttimes he falleth into the fire, and oft into the water. And I brought him to thy disciples, and they could not cure him.

Then Jesus answered and said, O faithless and perverse generation, how long shall I be with you? how long shall I suffer you? bring him hither to me. And Jesus rebuked the devil; and he departed out of him: and the child was cured from that very hour.

Then came the disciples to Jesus apart, and said, Why could not we cast him out? And Jesus said unto them, Because of your unbelief: for verily I say unto you, If ye have faith as a grain of mustard seed, ye shall say unto this mountain, Remove hence to yonder place; and it shall remove; and nothing shall be impossible unto you. Howbeit this kind goeth not out but by prayer and fasting.

Matthew 17:14-21

29. Healing the Ten Lepers

And it came to pass, as he went to Jerusalem, that he passed through the midst of Samaria and Galilee. And as he entered into a certain village, there met him ten men that were lepers, which stood afar off: And they lifted up their voices, and said, Jesus, Master, have mercy on us.

And when he saw them, he said unto them, Go shew yourselves unto the priests. And it came to pass, that, as they went, they were cleansed. And one of them, when he saw that he was healed, turned back, and with a loud voice glorified God, And fell down on his face at his feet, giving him thanks: and he was a Samaritan.

And Jesus answering said, Were there not ten cleansed? but where are the nine? There are not found that returned to give glory to God, save this stranger. And he said unto him, Arise, go thy way: thy faith hath made thee whole.

Luke 17:11-19

30. Healing the Blind Man

And as Jesus passed by, he saw a man which was blind from his birth. And his disciples asked him, saying, Master, who did sin, this man, or his parents, that he was born blind? Jesus answered, Neither hath this man sinned, nor his parents: but that the works of God should be made manifest in him.

I must work the works of him that sent me, while it is day: the night cometh, when no man can work. As long as I am in the world, I am the light of the world. When he had thus spoken, he spat on the ground, and made clay of the spittle, and he anointed the eyes of the blind man with the clay,

And said unto him, Go, wash in the pool of Siloam, (which is by interpretation, Sent.) He went his way therefore, and washed, and came seeing. The neighbours therefore, and they which before had seen him that he was blind, said, Is not this he that sat and begged?

Some said, This is he: others said, He is like him: but he said, I am he. Therefore said they unto him, How were thine eyes opened? He answered and said, A man that is called Jesus made clay, and anointed mine eyes, and said unto me, Go to the pool of Siloam, and wash: and I went and washed, and I received sight. Then said they unto him, Where is he? He said, I know not.

They brought to the Pharisees him that aforetime was blind. And it was the sabbath day when Jesus made the clay, and opened his eyes. Then again the Pharisees also asked him how he had received his sight. He said unto them, He put clay upon mine eyes, and I washed, and do see.

Therefore said some of the Pharisees, This man is not of God, because he keepeth not the sabbath day. Others said, How can a man that is a sinner do such miracles? And there was a division among them. They say unto the blind man again, What sayest thou of him, that he hath opened thine eyes? He said, He is a prophet.

But the Jews did not believe concerning him, that he had been blind, and received his sight, until they called the parents of him that had received his sight. And they asked them, saying, Is this your son, who ye say was born blind? how then doth he now see?

His parents answered them and said, We know that this is our son, and that he was born blind: But by what means he now seeth, we know not; or who hath opened his eyes, we know not: he is of age; ask him: he shall speak for himself. These words spake his parents, because they feared the Jews: for the Jews had agreed already, that if any man did confess that he was Christ, he should be put out of the synagogue.

Therefore said his parents, He is of age; ask him. Then again called they the man that was blind, and said unto him, Give God the praise: we know that this man is a sinner. He answered and said, Whether he be a sinner or no, I know not: one thing I know, that, whereas I was blind, now I see.

Then said they to him again, What did he to thee? how opened he thine eyes? He answered them, I have told you already, and ye did not hear: wherefore would ye hear it again? will ye also be his disciples? Then they reviled him, and said, Thou art his disciple; but we are Moses' disciples. We know that God spake unto Moses: as for this fellow, we know not from whence he is.

The man answered and said unto them, Why herein is a marvellous thing, that ye know not from whence he is, and yet he hath opened mine eyes. Now we know that God heareth not sinners: but if any man be a worshipper of God, and doeth his will, him he heareth. Since the world began was it not heard that any man opened the eyes of one that was born blind. If this man were not of God, he could do nothing.

They answered and said unto him, Thou wast altogether born in sins, and dost thou teach us? And they cast him out. Jesus heard that they had cast him out; and when he had found him, he said unto him, Dost thou believe on the Son of God? He answered and said, Who is he, Lord, that I might believe on him?

And Jesus said unto him, Thou hast both seen him, and it is he that talketh with thee. And he said, Lord, I believe. And he worshipped him. And Jesus said, For judgment I am come into this world, that they which see not might see; and that they which see might be made blind. And some of the Pharisees which were with him heard these words, and said unto him, Are we blind also? Jesus said unto them, If ye were blind, ye should have no sin: but now ye say, We see; therefore your sin remaineth.

John 9:1-41

31. Raising Lazarus

Now a certain man was sick, named Lazarus, of Bethany, the town of Mary and her sister Martha. (It was that Mary which anointed the Lord with ointment, and wiped his feet with her hair, whose brother Lazarus was sick.) Therefore his sisters sent unto him, saying, Lord, behold, he whom thou lovest is sick.

When Jesus heard that, he said, This sickness is not unto death, but for the glory of God, that the Son of God might be glorified thereby. Now Jesus loved Martha, and her sister, and Lazarus. When he had heard therefore that he was sick, he abode two days still in the same place where he was.

Then after that saith he to his disciples, Let us go into Judaea again. His disciples say unto him, Master, the Jews of late sought to stone thee; and goest thou thither again?

Jesus answered, Are there not twelve hours in the day? If any man walk in the day, he stumbleth not, because he seeth the light of this world. But if a man walk in the night, he stumbleth, because there is no light in him. These things said he: and after that he saith unto them, Our friend Lazarus sleepeth; but I go, that I may awake him out of sleep.

Then said his disciples, Lord, if he sleep, he shall do well. Howbeit Jesus spake of his death: but they thought that he had spoken of taking of rest in sleep. Then said Jesus unto them plainly, Lazarus is dead. And I am glad for your sakes that I was not there, to the intent ye may believe; nevertheless let us go unto him.

Then said Thomas, which is called Didymus, unto his fellow disciples, Let us also go, that we may die with him.

Then when Jesus came, he found that he had lain in the grave four days already. Now Bethany was nigh unto Jerusalem, about fifteen furlongs off: And many of the Jews came to Martha and Mary, to comfort them concerning their brother.

Then Martha, as soon as she heard that Jesus was coming, went and met him: but Mary sat still in the house. Then said Martha unto Jesus, Lord, if thou hadst been here, my brother had not died. But I know, that even now, whatsoever thou wilt ask of God, God will give it thee.

Jesus saith unto her, Thy brother shall rise again. Martha saith unto him, I know that he shall rise again in the resurrection at the last day. Jesus said unto her, I am the resurrection, and the life: he that believeth in me, though he were dead, yet shall he live: And whosoever liveth and believeth in me shall never die. Believest thou this?

She saith unto him, Yea, Lord: I believe that thou art the Christ, the Son of God, which should come into the world. And when she had so said, she went her way, and called Mary her sister secretly, saying, The Master is come, and calleth for thee. As soon as she heard that, she arose quickly, and came unto him.

Now Jesus was not yet come into the town, but was in that place where Martha met him. The Jews then which were with her in the house, and comforted her, when they saw Mary, that she rose up hastily and went out, followed her, saying, She goeth unto the grave to weep there. Then when Mary was come where Jesus was, and saw him, she fell down at his feet, saying unto him, Lord, if thou hadst been here, my brother had not died.

When Jesus therefore saw her weeping, and the Jews also weeping which came with her, he groaned in the spirit, and was troubled. And said, Where have ye laid him? They said unto him, Lord, come and see.

Jesus wept. Then said the Jews, Behold how he loved him! And some of them said, Could not this man, which opened the eyes of the blind, have caused that even this man should not have died? Jesus therefore again groaning in himself cometh to the grave. It was a cave, and a stone lay upon it.

Jesus said, Take ye away the stone. Martha, the sister of him that was dead, saith unto him, Lord, by this time he stinketh: for he hath been dead four days. Jesus saith unto her, Said I not unto thee, that, if thou wouldest believe, thou shouldest see the glory of God?

Then they took away the stone from the place where the dead was laid. And Jesus lifted up his eyes, and said, Father, I thank thee that thou hast heard me. And I knew that thou hearest me always: but because of the people which stand by I said it, that they may believe that thou hast sent me. And when he thus had spoken, he cried with a loud voice, Lazarus, come forth.

And he that was dead came forth, bound hand and foot with graveclothes: and his face was bound about with a napkin. Jesus saith unto them, Loose him, and let him go. Then many of the Jews which came to Mary, and had seen the things which Jesus did, believed on him. But some of them went their ways to the Pharisees, and told them what things Jesus had done.

John 11:1-46

32. Healing the Woman's Infirmity

And he was teaching in one of the synagogues on the sabbath. And, behold, there was a woman which had a spirit of infirmity eighteen years, and was bowed together, and could in no wise lift up herself. And when Jesus saw her, he called her to him, and said unto her, Woman, thou art loosed from thine infirmity. And he laid his hands on her: and immediately she was made straight, and glorified God.

And the ruler of the synagogue answered with indignation, because that Jesus had healed on the sabbath day, and said unto the people, There are six days in which men ought to work: in them therefore come and be healed, and not on the sabbath day. The Lord then answered him, and said, Thou hypocrite, doth not each one of you on the sabbath loose his ox or his ass from the stall, and lead him away to watering?

And ought not this woman, being a daughter of Abraham, whom Satan hath bound, lo, these eighteen years, be loosed from this bond on the sabbath day? And when he had said these things, all his adversaries were ashamed: and all the people rejoiced for all the glorious things that were done by him

Luke 13:10-17

33. Healing the Man With Dropsy

And it came to pass, as he went into the house of one of the chief Pharisees to eat bread on the sabbath day, that they watched him. And, behold, there was a certain man before him which had the dropsy. And Jesus answering spake unto the lawyers and Pharisees, saying, Is it lawful to heal on the sabbath day? And they held their peace. And he took him, and healed him, and let him go;

And answered them, saying, Which of you shall have an ass or an ox fallen into a pit, and will not straightway pull him out on the sabbath day? And they could not answer him again to these things.

Luke 14:1-6

34. Healing the Two Blind Men

And as they departed from Jericho, a great multitude followed him. And, behold, two blind men sitting by the way side, when they heard that Jesus passed by, cried out, saying, Have mercy on us, O Lord, thou son of David. And the multitude rebuked them, because they should hold their peace: but they cried the more, saying, Have mercy on us, O Lord, thou son of David.

And Jesus stood still, and called them, and said, What will ye that I shall do unto you? They say unto him, Lord, that our eyes may be opened. So Jesus had compassion on them, and touched their eyes: and immediately their eyes received sight, and they followed him.

Matthew 20:29-34

35. Cursing the Fig Tree

And on the morrow, when they were come from Bethany, he was hungry: And seeing a fig tree afar off having leaves, he came, if haply he might find any thing thereon: and when he came to it, he found nothing but leaves; for the time of figs was not yet. And Jesus answered and said unto it, No man eat fruit of thee hereafter for ever. And his disciples heard it.

Mark 11:12-14

36. Healing in the Temple

And the blind and the lame came to him in the temple; and he healed them.

Matthew 21:14

37. Healing the Servant's Ear

And one of them smote the servant of the high priest, and cut off his right ear. And Jesus answered and said, Suffer ye thus far. And he touched his ear, and healed him.

Luke 22:50,51

38. The Draught of Fishes

And he said unto them, Cast the net on the right side of the ship, and ye shall find. They cast therefore, and now they were not able to draw it for the multitude of fishes.

John 21:6

About the Author

R.W. Schambach is a bold, powerful, Holy Ghost revival preacher. For some forty years he has conducted evangelistic crusades in every major city in the United States and in many countries through-out the world.

R.W. Schambach's meetings are noted for enthusiastic worship, upbeat music, faith-building testimonies and challenging, Bible-based sermons. His demonstrative preaching style and down-to-earth practical messages have endeared him to thousands of people who have found inspiration, encouragement and deliverance in his services.

A trademark of the Schambach ministy is the large Gospel tent utilized for many of his city-wide and regional crusades. As large as a football field, the canvas cathedral attracts many who would never attend a typical church service. Schambach also uses large auditoriums and civic centers for crusades in some areas.

Rev. Schambach is a frequent television guest on the Trinity Broadcasting Network with Paul and Jan Crouch, and produces his own weekly telecast. His radio program, "Power Today," is broadcast daily throughout the United States and in 120 countries worldwide.

Despite graduating from seminary and having various degrees conferred upon him, he is known simply as "Brother" Schambach to those to whom he ministers. Brother Schambach has tremendous compassion for people, often laying hands on hundreds of people, praying for them one at a time long after his services have ended.

Missions is an important part of the Schambach ministry. In addition to helping build and provide ongoing support to an orphanage in Indonesia, the Schambach ministry has sponsored massive feeding programs in Haiti, disaster relief in Mexico and housing for Afghanistan refugees in Southeast Asia.

Rev. Schambach has personally conducted major open air crusades and meetings in several overseas countries, attracting some of the largest crowds ever assembled in the history of some nations. He preached to 50,000 each night in Georgetown, Guyana, where 25,000 made decisions for Christ and thousands more were healed and delivered through prayer.

Rev. Schambach ministered in Nigeria in 1981, preaching to capacity crowds in four major cities. Two years later, he held four days of services in a government-owned square in Laos, and 25,000 came to Christ.

In 1986, Rev. Schambach conducted a series of meetings through the West Indies. Crusades were conducted in Trinidad, Tobago, Grenada, Nevis, St. Kitts, Antigua and Puerto Rico attracting record crowds. In St. Kitts, authorities said the Schambach meeting had a much larger audience than Queen Elizabeth on her visit the previous year.

International headquarters for Schambach Revivals is located in Tyler, Texas. The ministry provides a 24-hour Power Phone, receiving calls from people requesting prayer for salvation, healing or other needs. POWER TODAY Magazine, published quarterly, is sent out to thousands of homes. Thousands of Rev. Schambach's sermons on video and audio cassettes and in book form are distributed each year.

R.W. Schambach and his wife, Mary Winifred, were married in 1948. They have three children.

To contact the author, write:
Schambach Revivals PO Box 9009 Tyler, Texas 75711
or call
(903)894-6141

Other Materials
By
POWER PUBLICATIONS

Books

By R.W. Schambach

You're One In A Million
Power For Victorious Christian Living
Four Lambs
Miracles: Eyewitness To The Miraculous
You Can't Beat God Givin'
What To Do When Trouble Comes
I Shall Not Want
The Secret Place
After The Fire
When You Wonder "Why?"
Power Of Faith For Today's Christian
Triumphant Faith
Power Struggle: Faith For Difficult Relationships
The R.W. Schambach Collection

By Donna Schambach

Tell, Teach & Train

By A.A. Allen

God's Guarantee To Heal You
The Price Of God's Miracle Working Power
Demon Possession Today And How To Be Free

Videos

By R.W. Schambach

Fabulous Fakes: *A Religion Of Form Vs. A Religion of Force*
Miracles
The Army Of The Lord
How To Raise The Dead
A Life Of Faith
Turn Up The Heat
Don't Touch That Dial
Break The Back Of Debt
Campmeeting With R.W. Schambach

Cassettes

By R.W. Schambach

(2) Tape Series
Fabulous Fakes: *A Religion Of Form Vs. A Religion of Force*
The Violent Take It By Force
Power Struggle
After The Fire
Shout

(4) Tape Series
Four Freedoms
A Little Bit Of The Bronx
Fear Not
Classics Of The Faith: *Classic Sermons On Faith & Power*

(6) Tape Series
When You Wonder "Why?"
The Tent Masters

(10) Tape Series
R.W. Schambach's Classic Sermons

By Donna Schambach

(2) Tape Series
How Does Healing Come?
The Dream Team

(3) Tape Series
Revival NOW

For more information about this ministry
and a free product catalog, please write:

SCHAMBACH REVIVALS, INC.
P O BOX 9009
TYLER, TX 75711

To order materials by phone, call:
(903)894-6141

WHEN YOU NEED PRAYER

Call the Power Phone

Every day of the week, 24 hours a day, a dedicated, faith-filled, Bible-believing prayer partner is ready to talk with you and pray about your needs. When you need prayer call:

(903)894-6141

If during the reading of this book, you made a decision to follow Christ, R.W. Schambach has a special gift for you. He has written a booklet that will help you continue growing in your new walk with God. It is called, *"You're One In a Million."* And, by simply writing or calling the ministry of Schambach Revivals and letting us know of your decision, we will mail this booklet to you, free of charge. Write or call:

Schambach Revivals
PO Box 9009
Tyler, TX 75711
(903) 894-6141